DAUGHTER OF THE RAZOR

PART II

THE RESCUE

Maria Tinschert

DAUGHTER OF THE RAZOR - PART II
THE RESCUE

First published in Australia by Maria Tinschert 2022

A catalogue record for this
book is available from the
National Library of Australia

ISBN: 978-0-9953977-2-9 (pbk)
ISBN: 978-0-9953977-3-6 (ebk)

Typesetting and design by Publicious Book Publishing
Published in collaboration with Publicious Book Publishing
www.publicious.com.au

This book is dedicated to my eldest son Dino, who likes to be called Dean. He was the dear little boy that Lyall hoped would die under a car, but he lived to become a loving son and a hardworking, fine, gentleman without crime, drugs or violence in his life. I am very proud of him, and he tells me every day that he is proud of his Mum.

Many have written about Sydney's 'Razor Gangs' and their criminal activities - there are numerous versions – but none are truer than a survivor's memories.

CONTENTS

PREFACE

I'm writing this book due to the popular demand that came from around the world after publication of 'Daughter of the Razor,' my first book. For me, it was an incredible feeling - a feeling of wonder - that people from other countries were so interested. They wanted to know if I had been rescued and what happened to me in later life. So, for those who haven't read my first book, I'll introduce myself. My name now is Maria Tinschert, born August 1932, but of course, my name was different then.

Named Mary Josephine Goodfield, I entered the world at 19 Sherbrooke Lane, Darlinghurst. In the middle of a depression, Sydney's run-down, inner-city houses had become slums where poor people with no work, lived in abject poverty. Many city-dwellers turned to crime as an economic necessity and my parents fitted into that category.

The house I was born in, a stone's throw from the 'red light' district, then in the heart of Australia's world of vice - the sly grog, the prostitution - the world where criminals from Melbourne joined the Sydney crime world. Later, my family moved to Sydney's outer suburb of Chullora, and my first book told of the horror - the criminal acts I lived through – and the cruelty, mostly at the hands of my family as well as others. It became my introduction to prostitution and as a young woman, my parents sold me into marriage. This in itself is a horror story, my story - 'Daughter of the Razor,' classified as restricted reading for obvious reasons. A lot of people found it confronting as I am very honest - if you write a true story, how can you doctor it or colour it to make it sound nice when it's not? Once you do that it is not really a true story.

So, it was graphic and pretty horrible, but I came to believe that it helped and inspired other people. Why? Because I am a survivor, and because I showed others that had also suffered through violence inflicted on them, not to allow people to tag them as a victim. I believe a victim is one that dies - they are survivors. If they weren't strong, they wouldn't be here. Us survivors, we haven't died, we are strong and tough, and here I am now at the age of eighty-nine. This is what it is about – it's about survival.

Now this second book will tell you how I was rescued at the age of twenty-nine. I am not good with dates - word association is the way I work. My first book comprised memories written from my many notes. A wonderful counsellor at Brisbane's Victims of Crime, whom I'm still in touch with, showed me how to write my memories.

We had settled in Queensland, Eberhard and I, and opened an antiques business, and everything went smoothly until I received a threatening phone call demanding money from a troubled female customer, to whom, in the past, I'd been quite kind, when she'd told me a sad story. I phoned the Redcliffe Police Station and talked to detectives who suggested this was extortion and that I agree to meet the woman in a public place. This I did, and they wired me up for sound. Eberhard drove me to the arranged meeting place at the Kippering Medical Centre whilst plain-clothes detectives mingled with the shoppers.

With a pounding heart, I left Eberhard in the car and walked slowly towards her. She was casually eating an apple outside the Centre. The woman, clasping a small cover - the size of a tooth-brush holder - in her hand, looked at me approaching and said, 'Did you bring me the money?' I answered that I had already given her some money to help her leave her husband -'Why are you asking for more, you foolish girl?'

She replied, 'Listen here, bitch, I still want more,' and flicked open the holder in her hand. Inside the holder, I saw the glint of what I thought was a knife as she lunged at me.

Petrified, I backed towards the car, and just in time, two plain-clothes police sprang into action, appearing out of the crowds. They quickly arrested her, but she plea-bargained her way out of a prison sentence as she was not carrying a knife – it was a letter-opener and not pre-mediated and walked free.

The case finalised, I was contacted by the Brisbane 'Victims of Crime' to assist me through my trauma. I resisted; I didn't feel it had been traumatic – after what I'd lived through it was just another of life's ordeals - but the counsellor persisted. Gradually, I found it helpful to talk about some of my own deep-seated sufferings from the years of horrifying abuse. She suggested I write it down as expressive writing is often used in therapeutic settings. It's helpful to victims to write about their ordeal. Over the next five years I did exactly that and those bits of hand-written paper became my first book.

This time I have no notes and must rely on what I remember. So, it will be a little bit different - sometimes I may jump around but it will be true, and it will show you that even though I had been rescued, it was not the fairy tales we read about, where the princess is rescued by the prince and lives happily ever after - it was not like that at all.

As a child, and until I turned twenty-nine, I was exceptionally backward, terribly uneducated, dreadfully inexperienced. When my father tapped on the side of his nose, I froze in terror. I had been taught to instantly do as I was told by the click of his fingers or by a whistle. I wasn't trained to think for myself, that I could do this or that. So being rescued was all very well, but it took me out of one sleazy situation into a difficult one. I was putty in the hands of the people out there, to be used or abused or whatever, not knowing whether something was right or wrong. If somebody said 'jump,' I just jumped - that's what I had been taught to do from a tot. So, I will tell you my story and what went on in those years. What happened to me and the family? I will reveal the tragic years I had to live through.

When I hear talk of all the good things God produced – the ocean, trees, mountains – I wonder what made him create the people in my early life - to what purpose? When I went into that marriage with Lyall at seventeen, I thought … I hoped … in my mixed-up mind … that it would prove to be a better life than the one I lived in - the hell and torment at the hands of my own family. I never expected it to be the same or worse.

Thinking back, I can still hear Lyall's mother, Mrs Buchanan, singing hymns around the house. I wonder how Lyall's family, Salvation Army members, could think they were Christians yet be so non religious, so money-hungry and cruel to me and my little ones. As it turned out, they were hiding behind their religion. I shake my head when I think back to how I trusted Joyce, Lyall's sister. I thought she was on my side when she sympathised - 'Lyall is so bad.' Many years older than me, and at the time I thought wiser, Joyce was as bad as the rest of that family.

I learned that life was nothing like they told me it would be. When I was rescued, I thought everything would change for the better but, as I explain in this book, you will see that I found life is not what I thought. 'Life' is what happened, what I did and what I felt - there were so many things I had to learn - I had to learn to feel. Yes, 'to feel' - I will say it again, 'to feel.' Even to feel my own judgement, to feel my own heart, to feel my own everything. I learned that what one feels, what one senses, is generally the only thing to trust. Our senses are so finely tuned to the universe, but we are not aware of it - not realising that our body is our God and our only God, because it is you - it is yours, it's nobody else's, it's strictly yours. So, life went on.

In the book I talk about the cruelty, the slavery of my life. The knowledge I did not have then, shows me what a slave I was. I will not say 'what a fool,' because I had been brought up to believe that I was there to DO - nothing more.

* * *

CHAPTER 1

FINDING MY ANGEL

As I think about this second part of my story, I want you to come along with me in my telling, as people did with my first book, not to inflict pain on you but for you to understand what it really meant to grow up and survive two terrible families. I was Mary, born into one family and, at seventeen, sold into the second and in both they tortured and abused me physically, mentally, and verbally, and used me as a slave.

Now that I'm Maria, I often cry for Mary. She never cried – she didn't know how to cry – she had disassociated herself from emotion years ago. She didn't know much at all. I cry for the love Mary never had as a child and, with so many appalling things happening to her, I often wonder what kept Mary alive through all the horror? Well, I will tell you – I think a picture helped me though.

The nuns gave me a print of a guardian angel, hovering over two little children. At my first school St Jerome's in Punchbowl, they gave me a long veil and I took holy communion, although I had no idea what was happening at the time. The nuns handed out pictures, knowing it would shut the kids up I suppose, but I feel now that the picture of the holy angel actually helped – it gave me hope. In the print, two children were sheltered from the chasm in front of them by an angel. I kept waiting for the angel to come and save me. As a child, I felt I never fitted in and, from time to time, I needed an angel. I made excuses for the angel's non-appearance – too busy looking after the two in the picture or something like that - but I knew the guardian angel would eventually come to save me. Well, guess what? In my eighties I actually found my angel and the angel found me.

In Queensland's Elanora Library one afternoon, I came across this dainty blonde apparition, unlike the tall slim angel in the print. To me she looked about thirty and had a sweet and gentle manner and a musical, soothing voice.

After a short exchange, she ushered me to a quiet part of the library, and we sat and talked about my life and the difficulties I had writing it. I discovered she worked for the library, and was knowledgeable, and aware of things happening in the world - as aware of me as I was of her. She felt passionately that my incredible story should be told to help others who had suffered and gave me advice and guidance. Without her I would not have written the first book and my secrets would have remained secrets I carried with me.

I had an odd feeling of safety meeting this angel – now don't think I've lost the plot. A psychologist told me I am certainly of sound mind and have an excellent memory but, in my eighties, I finally found my angel. This angel has a name – Anna. The name suits her –'Anna the Angel.' So Elanora Library can be very proud they have an angel.

* * *

CHAPTER 2

MARRIAGE TO LYALL

The Buchanan family, with whom I spent so many terrible years, were well-known as members of The Salvation Army, in Sydney's Strathfield area. Mrs Buchanan had divorced her husband years before and she ruled the roost. Her boarder, live-in lover Jack Borrowdale, her son Lyall and daughter Joyce - with her two small daughters - all of them were under Mrs Buchanan's control; none had the courage to stand up to her. She had accumulated powerful friends and built a facade of Christian respectability.

I had once thought Joyce was my salvation, but I really can't blame her for letting me down as her mother commanded the household. I saw early on that her son followed his mother's every word.

My mother and Mrs Buchanan were introduced through a lady who lived near my parents - a member of The Salvation Army who knew Mrs Buchanan; she presented herself as an established and committed Christian. This pillar of society had a single, uncouth, awkward son called Lyall. My parents knew from the magistrate (as described in my first book) I was too naïve to look after myself, alone, out in the workforce – but old enough to let family secrets slip out, and they didn't want that to happen. My father wanted rid of me at home; to my family I was just a commodity. They had already tried to palm me off with an obese man, but he'd become too drunk, so when the Buchanans came along, it became the perfect opportunity for them to rid themselves of me where I could do no harm – to sell me to this family – so for six hundred pounds Lyall's family took me off his hands.

At seventeen I was a tall, slim, attractive girl with olive skin and dark, curly shoulder-length hair. Lyall's mother, Mrs Buchanan, obviously thought if she bought a wife for her son, she would also add a slave to her household. Shy, and immature, I only met my future husband once prior to the wedding. I had no say in the matter anyway … I had been sold into slavery.

One rainy day, petrified with fear, I married Lyall Buchanan at the Baptist Church in Burwood. I wasn't consulted about anything - his mother hurriedly arranged everything, even giving me a hat, shoes, and a pale blue outfit to wear to the ceremony; I reluctantly agreed to everything I was asked. I didn't know I had an option.

Lyall wore a pin-stripe suit. He looked quite unattractive - a plain, skinny looking guy, of medium height with ugly teeth, big sticking-out ears, no personality, and a gambling habit – one of the reasons why Mrs Buchanan bought her uncouth son a wife, was that nobody else would want him. My parents attended, casually sitting at the back of the church, my father wearing a bow tie and smoking a cigar, with his feet up on a pew, eager to ensure the deal went through. Us newlyweds – strangers really – spent the wedding night sleeping together on the Buchanan's Strathfield veranda opposite the toilet door.

I soon saw Lyall was a sexual pervert addicted to gambling, and Mrs Buchanan was not the religious, law-abiding matriarch she portrayed. Employed at Farmers, a city store, she often returned home after work with dozens of pairs of stolen silk stockings concealed in her underwear to sell later.

I realised just how much power Mrs Buchanan wielded, when she informed me I would be going to a ball where the Chief of Police would be present. Dressed for the evening in a beautiful white gown, with all the extras, which Mrs Buchanan borrowed, I was told to keep my mouth shut. Joyce was also dressed in a gorgeous blue gown and Lyall wore a suit, and they came with me.

We were collected in a car by Eric, a policeman friend of Mrs Buchanan, and driven to Sydney Harbour's Circular Quay. There we joined the upper echelon of the New South Wales police for a ball on 'The Kalang Showboat' – a vehicular ferry used between Sydney's north and south shores. That night it had been hired by the Police Federation for a ball. Lyall and Joyce kept a close eye on me, but it took me years to understood this was my mother-in-law's way of showing her police friends, the 'merchandise' she had for hire. However, at the time, it clearly showed me who Mrs Buchanan's friends were and explained why she could hold gambling meetings and not be raided.

Unable to think for myself; the Buchanans completely controlled me – mind and body - and I had no say in anything. No-one asked me anything or listened anyway and Lyall physically threatened me into silence. I became pregnant to Lyall, and when my baby was born, my mother-in-law named her Michele Buchanan. Mrs Buchanan continually told me Michele wasn't mine - the family would keep Michele - insisting 'the little blonde girl belongs to the Buchanans – she's Lyall's' and hearing this filled me with fear. However, Lyall had no interest in his daughter whatsoever, never even nursing her as a baby.

One time, in desperation, I took baby Michele, wrapped in a shawl in my arms, and went to my mother's house. She saw me through a window, opened the front door and quickly shut it after telling me good money had changed hands for me and to go back to Lyall, as I was 'owned by the Buchanans now.'

I did all the housework and cooking in the Buchanan's house (I don't know where I learned all this), and from the start, Lyall was physically violent. Even worse, he traded me to men, and I had no say in the matter. He settled his gambling debts by using me sexually, while he watched us. I didn't argue – this was the way I'd been raised, not to argue. I had no opinion – my parents had broken my will when I was a child. I was too afraid of them to argue. I was a slave living in plain sight but everyone in the

Buchanan household turned a 'blind-eye' to the men who came to the house. However, when I became pregnant to one of the men, Lyall knew his mother wouldn't be happy, and she pulled the strings. I began to worry about what lay ahead as she'd already told me how she had aborted unwanted babies in the past.

Unbeknown to me, Mrs Buchanan had taken over and arranged everything with The Salvation Army seniors. Years later I discovered Lyall, and my names, were omitted as parents from the birth certificate and Lyall had written on the adoption form that I was an Afro-Indian who didn't speak English.

The day after baby Melissa was born, Lyall collected me and my daughter from the hospital, and we took the baby to a Salvation Army house in Stanmore. They probably wanted to check her over. I didn't understand what was happening or panic as we were to collect her next day. The following morning we returned to The Salvation Army home and collected her – then continued on to a city Sydney solicitor; I didn't know why. In the office, the receptionist opened her arms for the new-born. I thought she was about to admire her, but she walked away carrying the baby. Lyall clicked his fingers, motioning me to follow, and we left the office without the baby.

Despite my dazed bewilderment - I was weak and hazy from giving birth - Lyall hustled me out the door and back to the railway station. I never saw my baby girl again and no-one talked about the baby after that. I had no living skills and couldn't cry. I had stopped crying very early in my life to prevent further punishment and give my tormentors the satisfaction of knowing they'd hurt me. My little baby was forgotten – but not by me. I resented the family for not wanting my little girl and giving her away, but I was their slave – I had no say in anything. From my early years, I had been made aware than nobody took any notice of me, and anyway, I had no rights, and no-one cared. I was an on-call servant, twenty-four hours a day. This was the way I'd been raised, not to think or asked questions but to obey. If my family had told me to commit a murder, there is no doubt in my mind I would have done it - to please them. I did whatever I was told to do. I had been raised to never resist them and keep my pain from view. In silence I mourned my loss and carried an ache inside me for thirty-fours years until I found her.

Joyce, my sister-in-law, who was years older than me, and a married woman with two small children, slyly agreed her brother treated me badly and I deserved better. Little did I know that a plan had been hatched among the Buchanan clan. Joyce, herself a woman of loose morals, told me about Tony. He was an older man, a tall, handsome, heavy-set Italian who, unbeknown to me, had married an Italian woman by proxy, in a phone call to Italy. Apparently, the plan was his Italian bride would join him in Australia later but in the meantime, he needed female companionship. I didn't understand that I was being hired out to him for sex.

To Tony and the Buchanans, this was just another transaction. He paid Lyall a regular income – but, at that time, to me Tony was a sanctuary from loneliness in a house where I was treated as a nobody – a lesser person. Friendly and quite kind, Tony would come to the house often and we had sex. No-one ever indicated that this way of life was wrong – not my husband, his family or anyone - it was all accepted in the Buchanan house. Soon I became pregnant and delivered Tony's son. Although Tony knew he was the father, my son was given the Buchanan surname. It preserved the pretence, to the outside world, that the Buchanans ran a normal household.

Tony's child was beautiful, with olive skin and dark curly hair but Tony took no notice of his son. My life was full of bad men and violence. I spent many days in pain and had quite a few hospitalisations from this existence … Lyall's gambling debts had become enormous, and I was the one who paid the debts with my body. Over the next few years, Tony continued to be a frequent visitor, and he knew he was their father when I gave birth to another two sons. All taking the Buchanan surname, Tony's three boys had Italian looks – olive skin, brown eyes, and dark brown hair. Mrs Buchanan, in her threats, often grumbled that having children with Tony was grounds for divorce and Lyall could easily divorce me, put me out on the street, any time he liked, but of course the family would keep his fair-skinned, blonde daughter.

'She's a REAL Buchanan.'

I now had four children living with me - Lyall's blonde daughter Michele was the eldest, four years older than the next child, and three sons who looked like Tony. Whilst the children saw Lyall as their father, he completely ignored them, and, like me, they feared his moods. Unlike Lyall, Tony spoke kindly to the children but never brought them presents or petted them. To him his three sons just didn't exist as his own children – they were part of the Buchanan household.

Tony never made any promises or spoke endearingly, but sometimes chatted, telling me titbits about his life. I suppose I hoped I would eventually fit into Tony's life somewhere, despite being married to Lyall. *Maybe he'll take me and the children away from these awful Buchanans, and we'll live happily.* I didn't think it through and asked for nothing more than just existing. All I ever wanted was a simple life without violence and Lyall's male 'visitors.' In my twenties, this hard life had taken a toll on my health, and I suffered in silence, but I lived for my children.

From time to time, Tony confided details of his house, implying that I would like it. In my naïve way I thought he meant that, at some time in the future, I would be living there with him - despite the fact that I was legally married to Lyall. It gave me hope.

After a few years even Mrs Buchanan had concerns about Lyall. He worked as a truck driver but being a heavy gambler, was always being chased for debts. She and her daughter Joyce were both petty thieves, stealing from their employers, but worried that Lyall's many gambling debts would bring them all undone - the police might raid the house and involve them. Joyce had been working at Jantzen's swim-wear factory and been caught stealing. Mrs Buchanan told Lyall his unpaid debts were creating problems and would eventually bring the police calling. She didn't want her reputation sullied in the area where they considered her 'a lady.' She continued to warn Lyall, and eventually directed him (and therefore me and the children,) to leave.

'Lyallie, you have to go' she ordered.

Her boarder Jack Borrowdale must have used his influence with his well-placed friends as, within a short time, a government-owned brick cottage, was found for us in the suburb of Villawood. Without my knowledge (I didn't have any say in anything - I was always told what to think) Lyall had visited Waltons, a large store, and filled the empty house with furniture.

Because he lost his truck-driving job, the only work Lyall could find was driving and he found a job driving taxi cabs. I overheard him talking gleefully about this wonderful job opportunity to a male friend who visited the house. He was excited about the chance of women being unable to pay the fare and him being paid 'in kind.' When he was asked about me and the children he replied how he didn't give a s**t and that he would find me a job, which he did. It was a few hours at night, cooking food at a nearby drive-in theatre. Lyall had arranged for the sweet woman who lived next door, to baby-sit the sleeping children whilst I worked. That money was supposed to keep me and the children as Lyall only gave me two shillings per day to feed us all. I became resourceful with eking the food and made sure the children ate as well as I could. With so little money, I ate less and less until many days I ate nothing and starved.

Driving a taxi suited Lyall and never once did he miss his family. He never referred to his mother or sister, despite that I later found his mother would give him money to gamble … that's what he did on different shifts when he was supposed to be driving. Our only visitor to the house was Tony.

One day, when the eldest two children were at school, I set off to see Tony's house – somehow, I knew the address. To this day I don't know what made me do it, especially as I suffered from agoraphobia, but I was determined. It took two trains, a bus and a lot of walking. With one little boy by my side and the baby in my arms, we arrived at Tony's house and knocked on the door. Tony opened the door himself and gave a surprised, sheepish grin when he saw me, with the children, standing on his doorstep.

'What are you doing here' he asked, surprised?

'I've come to have a look' I answered.

His only questions were how I got there, and who gave me the fare. He didn't even glance at the children as he enquired 'so … it's a nice house, isn't it? Do you like it?'

Although I wasn't interested in houses, I agreed and, since he didn't invite me in, I stepped across the threshold. Inside he reluctantly took me around, eventually showing me a bedroom. On the bedside table I noticed a photo of a new-born baby with a purple mark down its face.

'Whose baby is that' I asked in surprise?

'Mine' he replied, grinning. 'My wife is still in hospital. Our baby was born a few days ago.'

I wasn't emotional – I wasn't used to showing emotion, it had never been allowed – but I felt crushed. This new feeling slowly turned to annoyance. Astonished, I asked 'You have a wife? This is your baby? I didn't know you were married.'

He shrugged and replied 'Everybody knew. We were married by proxy over the phone to Italy. Joyce knew, the Buchanans knew, everybody knew.'

'I didn't know' I muttered, overcome by a feeling of misery.

Dispassionately, he replied 'You didn't have to know. Lyall is the boss - Lyall got his money. You didn't ever fight before this.'

Fight? I thought? *Fight? – in my position? There's no point in putting up a fight. I'm not allowed to fight, am I?*

Something inside me shifted. It dawned on me that, all these years, everyone knew Tony had a wife … except for me. She must have come to Australia recently - that same year since her baby was almost a similar age as mine. I saw that my ideas of a future life with him were just fantasy and the Buchanans had set me up. I felt humiliated, and for the first time, an unfamiliar angry feeling grew as I started to move towards the front door.

'Where are you going'?' he asked as I hesitated on the doorstep outside. 'Don't be stupid now.'

For the first time I looked him straight in the eye and replied 'Don't you ever … ever…come near me again and don't think that you and Lyall are the boss.'

I walked away shocked - angry, confused and hurt - returning home in time for the two children to come home from school. I didn't cry, I never cried in those days, but I felt so used and thoroughly miserable. I didn't have an outburst at home, but it played on my mind that Tony kept a photo of a baby with a birth mark at his bedside. *He's never taken a photo of my beautiful baby boys* and all my dreams and hopes for the future were in shreds. Everything Joyce had suggested concerning a future with Tony and leaving Lyall – it had all been lies - a made-up fairy story to soothe me. I also realised Tony had no heart … no soul … he was just like my gambling, money-grabbing husband.

I said nothing to Lyall about my visit, but he found out I'd visited Tony – how, I don't know as, at the time, communication wasn't easy, unlike today with mobile phones. A few days later, Lyall came in and confronted me. Standing over me he hollered, 'What right have you got - to go to Tony's place and put on a show?'

I replied that I hadn't put on a show.

'Well, why did you go?'

'I wanted to look at my house' I replied.

'Your house? he roared in astonishment.

I answered that Joyce had given me to understand Tony would be taking me to the house to live and I wanted to look at it. His reply was his usual put-down. 'For a dummy, you hear a lot of things, don't you? You're gonna be in a lot of trouble. You'd better change your mind about Tony coming here.'

I replied that I wouldn't, but he became menacing and insisted I would.

I was beginning to feel complete despair at the thought of this life continuing. However, there was nowhere for a distressed woman to go in those days. I did complain once about my life to a policeman at Burwood Police Station. He asked me if my husband had a job and when I nodded, he told me to get myself home to my hard-working husband who provided for his family, and not to bother the police with my whinging ... not come to them every time things got tough. If a woman complained about abuse, the welfare people would come to the house, report on the situation, and take the children away. The children would be split up and the mother had no rights. She could not see them or have her children returned – I wasn't prepared to deal with that. I had beautiful children and they were the only things I ever had, that I could love. They were my family, and I loved them fiercely. I wasn't willing to lose them. I sometimes sat on a chair and observed them in wonder. At night I watched them sleep, they looked so adorable – the loves of my life and the best thing that God did for me – my living breathing dolls.

Unexpectedly one day, when our eldest son was about five and Lyall was home, he took him for a walk down the road to the shop. This was a short walk to Miller Road, a main thoroughfare with heavy peak-hour traffic. I should have been suspicious as it was extremely unusual for Lyall to bother with the children, but I wasn't alarmed until I heard the sound of ambulance sirens and people outside yelling my name – my son had been hurt. Lyall had given the little boy a six-penny coin and sent him into the traffic, across the road to the sweetshop. Lyall then stood on the footpath and watched the truck hit him.

My neighbour took care of the children at home, I rushed to Miller Street and ran towards the commotion. I found my little boy being lifted into the ambulance; they sat me in the front and took off for Fairfield Hospital ... where I waited. My boy was unconscious and placed in the Intensive Care ward. Whilst waiting, I was approached by a couple of nuns. They told me they would pray for me, but it meant nothing to me – like the angel picture. I was petrified for my son and didn't understand what was happening.

Much later that night, a policeman who had attended the accident and who lived in my street, gave me a lift home. He told me he was at a loss to understand how my son had wandered so far from home as he had never seen my children playing in the street. I didn't explain but I knew Lyall's dreadful intention.

But he didn't succeed … my boy's alive. However, I remained concerned as he had severe injuries and his head had swollen. Fortunately, he survived and came home, where I helped him to walk and talk again, but whilst recovering from being hit by the truck, his health remained frail, and he developed a terrible cough.

Gradually his cough became worse, affecting his breathing. So I took him to Mr Lamonte, the nearest chemist, who told me to get him to hospital. He said 'I can't give you anything that will help – it's a lung infection and the Coast Hospital in Kurnell is the best place for him. They specialise in these things.'

I had no idea where Kurnell was, so I rushed him to the only person I knew who might help, Dr Egan. He repeated my son needed to go to the Coast Hospital. Despite my husband driving a taxi, he wasn't around and wouldn't have been interested anyway, so we made the long trek by walking, buses, and trains to Kurnell. With directions in hand, the journey seemed to take an eternity. The hospital staff examined my little boy and indeed, agreed my son had a lung infection. They kept him there and I had no choice but to return home alone.

Back home I knew I couldn't do the long journey every day, and Lyall wasn't concerned or interested, but I desperately wanted to know how my boy was. I spoke to Mr Lamonte the chemist and asked how on earth I could find out about my son's progress. He must have seen how worried and helpless I was and offered a solution. I would visit the chemist once a day and could use his phone to contact the hospital. That night. Lyall didn't ask why I seemed so utterly miserable, why my boy wasn't at home – he didn't care about anybody but himself and just left for work next morning.

The weeks passed and my son recovered. Released from the hospital again, I nursed him back to health and he eventually returned to school. He grew up to be a wonderful man, but he suffered with health problems for many years after Lyall's attempt on his life.

* * *

I continued to act like a slave, doing the housework and caring for the children. When I cleaned the house, I took the children into each room with me, and one morning whilst cleaning the bathroom, a bottle of PineOCleen, sitting on the end of the bath rim, fell into the bath and the glass bottle broke. The lid, attached to part of the broken bottle, shot out and hit my hand, the glass cutting deep into the flesh. Blood spurted everywhere, which set off the children, crying and frightened at the sight of blood. The noise of screaming caught the attention of my neighbour who came rushing into the house. When she saw the bloody state of the bathroom and that the bleeding wouldn't stop, she scooped us up, the children and me, and took us to the nearby doctor. Dr Egan dressed my cut hand and told me I should get in touch with the company who made PineOCleen, he felt the design was dangerous, being in a breakable glass bottle, and suggested I contact the makers and ask for compensation.

I shook my head, telling him I couldn't do that. He insisted I would get compensation, but after being pressed to explain, I admitted any money would only go to my husband. Dr Egan offered to have the money addressed to him for my collection, but I continued to shake my head. He could see something was not quite right with my household; the children looked well but I looked under-nourished and could see I had bruised arms. He kept pressing me for answers, but the 'code of silence' was so entrenched in me, I couldn't explain and left quickly.

I had to return a couple of times to have the dressings replaced and each time the doctor asked me to contact the manufacturers, explaining the compensation money might be enough to get me out on my own. I had no intention of doing this or telling him anything – it was a private matter, and I knew I would suffer if Lyall found I had extra money. I didn't know until later that, on race days, my husband was gambling and not working. I found that when he had no money, his mother would hock things to give him funds, cementing his gambling habit.

A week later a furniture truck pulled up outside the house and a man knocked at our front door. I opened it and he said 'I'm from Waltons. Did your old man buy a load of furniture from Waltons?'

I agreed and he replied 'I need to come in. He hasn't made a payment and we're here to repossess everything.'

So I stood aside and watched as they took all the furniture, everything … the beds, sofa, table, chairs, refrigerator … out the door and loaded it into the van. I told them I thought my husband had paid but they just smiled and ignored me whilst commenting on how nice I'd kept all the pieces. My distressed next-door neighbour saw this happening and came running in to ask what had happened.

'What you gonna do?'

I had no idea and told her I'd make up beds on the floor for the children, but she felt sorry for us – that we had nothing to sit on – and brought in two old chairs from her house. When Lyall came home at the end of a shift, he looked around and saw the empty house. I explained the furniture had been repossessed. His only comment was 'They're bloody swift, aren't they?'

We were all sleeping on the floor, but Lyall wasn't troubled – certainly not about us, the children or me having nowhere to sleep or eat. He was only interested in dodging the people to whom he owed money. He was a good-for-nothing deviate, a terrible gambler and a bad loser and owed enormous debts to people who could have done us harm. At the time I didn't realise how deadly it might have become. These people could have taken it out on me and the children, thinking it would affect Lyall. But it wouldn't have – it wouldn't have hurt him one bit – he would have been only too pleased to be let off the hook for his debts.

From time to time, I had to visit Dr Egan as I had on-going appointments to take my son – follow-ups on the terrible injuries he's received in the traffic incident. The next time, after attending to him, the doctor informed me he had written to the PineOCleen company and received my compensation money from the incident.

'I don't think the PineOCleen people will be using glass for much longer,' he explained as he continued to ask me to consider taking the money. Just so I could get away from his prying eyes, I told him I'd think about it. He could see that I looked unwell, deprived of food, and I knew he would soon start to question me. As I ushered my two children outside, I felt a tap on my shoulder. When I turned around, I saw the person responsible was a small blonde woman.

'It's Mary, isn't it?' she asked. 'You went to St Theresa's School. I went there too; don't you remember me? I'm Patricia - I used to live down the road to the school.'

She smiled and I saw she had two deep dimples …*yes, I do remember a little blonde girl who had dimples at the school.*

'Are these your children?' she asked. 'They're beautiful.'

After all these years … yes, I do remember her. I told her I had another two at home with a neighbour.

'Goodness' was her surprised reply.

I had never met anyone who knew me from school before. 'Do you live near here?' I asked, as surprised as she was.

'No, but I come here all the time to visit friends nearby.' She continued, 'I've never forgotten you, you know, Mary. I always felt you had troubles at home. When I told my sister about you, she said there was a lot of problems in your house, but I never forgot you … we should meet and catch up. Can I come and visit you?'

I bit my lip and felt uncomfortable – I'd never had a friend, never had anyone Lyall didn't know visit before, and this felt dangerous.

'Dunno' … I never have visitors.'

She persisted, asking my address and I gave it to her. Then I panicked. 'You can't come tomorrow.'

'Why not?'

'My husband might be home,' I replied quickly.

She seemed to understand my fright, and we settled on a day I knew Lyall wouldn't be at the house. I returned home - the question uppermost in my mind was *have I done the right thing? How will this work out?*

* * *

CHAPTER 3

PATRICIA'S VISITS

The day of Patricia's visit, I wondered how things would be between us. When I thought hard about it, I did vaguely remember her from school. A sweet, dimpled girl, she was gentle and always dressed in neat, clean clothes and her blonde hair was soft and brushed. I remember she had older sisters because she had talked about them, but she never asked me questions. *Fancy - now we're both women … and she still remembers me!* I hoped it was for the right reasons.

The time we had agreed upon arrived, and I looked out the window and saw her at the gate. She looked so neat and dainty – she wore a pretty dress and carried a handbag. I heard her shoes clip clop up the path, followed by a gently tap on the door. I opened it, greeted her and our footsteps echoed in the empty house as I took her into the lounge where we sat down on the only furniture in the empty room, two shabby chairs.

'You told me you had four children, so I bought them a present - two apples and two oranges,' she said offering me a paper bag. I noticed she wasn't looking around at the emptiness but focussed on me as she continued. 'Who would have believed we would meet up after all these years Mary, and so far away from where we went to school.'

I nodded in agreement and explained, apart from St Theresa and St Jerome, I had never attended another school. She continued, recalling seeing me on my first day there.

'You looked so nice, and I liked your hair – you still have those lovely curls' – there was still no word from her about the missing furniture.

I showed her my two youngest children who were napping, on the temporary beds I'd made on the bedroom floor. We were all sleeping on the floor, not that Lyall cared. His focus was dodging the people to whom he owed money. He was a worthless person, a terrible gambler and a bad loser and had enormous, unsettled debts to people who could have done us harm.

Patricia and I tiptoed in and stood admiring the toddlers as they slept. She looked quite sad and whispered she thought they were beautiful with their black curls. We went back to the lounge room, to the chairs, and continued talking. This time Patricia was almost in tears, telling me her own personal story.

'I have a son too Mary, but I committed a terrible sin. About a year ago at Christmas, I left my husband because he was a nasty brute … but I had to leave my son with him. There's nowhere to go to when you have a child – my mother and older sisters have all gone and I had no-one to turn to.'

I questioned if leaving got her into trouble, and she shook her head and gave me a puzzled expression. 'Trouble?'

'Didn't your husband come after you?' I asked.

'No, he wouldn't have dared. I'd have called the police and he knew it would be the end for him … but I had no-one to turn to. I left with just one bag. He wasn't rough with our son. He loves him but I had to go. Now I have a tiny place of my own and I work shift-work at a factory … and I knit to fill my spare time. Do you knit Mary?'

'No … I don't know how,' I replied and, when she asked me how things were with me, I thought what can I tell her? *How can I tell her my story? She's so different to me. I can't I tell her the truth – she's had such a normal, protected upbringing. She'll never understand.*

She took my hand and said, 'Trust me, Mary … trust me.'

I knew I didn't look well. Lyall had fractured my jaw and my mouth was slightly twisted and swollen. I knew from my reflection in the tiny bathroom mirror that I looked terribly thin. I was a person with no mind to speak of. How could I tell this sweet, dimpled person what type of life I led? I didn't cry – I didn't feel emotional enough to make me cry. Any such reaction had been beaten out of me years ago.

For the very first time, here was somebody who actually seemed to care about me. In my heart I felt it and I caved in and couldn't stop myself. Some of my story poured out – but not everything. The 'code of silence' ensured I didn't tell all, but I told her how I'd been sold to Lyall - money had been paid for me and so I belonged to him. I explained how my second baby girl had been taken away to The Salvation Army home by the Buchanan family. I saw the look of amazement on her face as I revealed just a little of my life. She wanted to know why my family hadn't come to save me and I explained it was my family that had sold me, they didn't want me. My mother didn't want me around. I was too old.

She looked bewildered. 'Why?'

'Well, as I grew older, my parents didn't want me there. I might have talked. I might have told people about my life, our life, how we lived and how they made their money. They didn't want me to tell anyone. So … when someone suggested Lyall's Salvation Army family might want a wife for their single son, arrangements were made, and a large amount of money changed hands.'

Patricia looked dumbfounded and had trouble understanding my tale of woe. 'So … they sold you? … Did you want to? … really … they must have known what they did to you was wrong. I remember you had older brothers. Didn't they know and come to help?'

I told her about my brothers, especially Goody. I explained how he'd threatened me from childhood, that he planned to kill me and boasted he would never go to jail for it. 'They're as bad as each other – they're evil. Especially Goody.' He didn't live far away, and I always feared he might come … *and then my children would have no mother.*

I started to tremble as I remembered I shouldn't be talking about the family.

'I shouldn't …there's great punishment – great punishment – if I talk.'

Stunned, Patricia tried to absorb the horror of my life. 'Did you ever love him … Lyall, I mean?

I stayed silent as I struggled to understand her question, then said 'I don't think so. I didn't know him. Arrangements were made.'

'Did you want to marry him?' Patricia asked.

I shrugged my shoulders. 'I was told to marry him. I HAD to. My parents sold me to the Buchanans. I belong to them.'

'I don't understand - you were sold … sold? You had no choice? Aw … that's terrible …' Patricia looked round the room and continued … 'Mary, what happened here? Why do you have no furniture? Why are you living like this?'

I felt odd talking about it … *this is wrong. I shouldn't be talking … I've never talked about it before.*

…'well …um … Lyall didn't pay Walton's for it, and they came and took everything away.'

'Oh Mary, what a life … and oh …you look so thin. I can see you're not well. How can your neighbours see this and let this happen? How can your husband let this go on?'

'Huh' I mumbled. 'People don't want to get involved Patricia. They turn their backs and pretend it's not their business. Lots of people have an idea what's happening, but no-one helps me.'

When she suggested going to the police, I panicked and had told her the story of my baby daughter being taken by The Salvation Army. I knew she understood something bad was happening, knew she wanted to help me, but I also knew that when she left, I had no protection. I would be on my own.

With a heavy heart I continued, 'I haven't asked for help. Anyway, nobody wants to help me – not the police – nobody. I'm trapped … maybe until we're all dead.'

Patricia looked appalled. 'The doctor sees you … does he know? Mary, you have to trust me. Does he know?'

I shrugged and explained I hadn't told him anything, but I'd been seeing him as my hand needed attention. I showed her my hand and explained the accident and how the doctor had written to the company, and they had paid compensation and the doctor had received it, not keeping the money himself, but for me – but if I took the money, I knew Lyall would gamble it away and be furious that I'd kept it a secret from him.

Patricia tried to take in the reality of the terrible life I'd was leading. She knew I hadn't told her everything and continued to ask me to trust her, promising she wouldn't tell anyone, but I couldn't open up. *It's a family matter so I can't ever tell anyone* – Lyall would be very angry and then I'd be in even more trouble.

Dismayed, Patricia replied 'Oh Mary, are you eating? I can see you're not well. This can't go on – doesn't anyone care?'

I shrugged. Some days the pains were worse than others, but I couldn't tell her. *How can I tell her?*

She asked how much money the doctor was holding for me, and I told her three thousand pounds. Her eyes widened. Astounded, she looked at me and told me I had enough to start again – I should leave.

'But where will I go? I have four children. I can't go anywhere.'

She shook her head, a worried look on her face but she understood the emotional cage of fear I lived in. The afternoon seemed to have flown by and it was time for me to collect the children from the school bus, but she wanted to stay and call the police right then and there. Terrified, I refused. I knew I would pay an even bigger price - they would take my children away. I knew only too well that Mrs Buchanan had friends in the police force.

Patricia insisted she wanted to do more for me, and we agreed she would visit me again, but she promised not to tell anyone – especially not the police.

When she came the next time, she could see I was in a bad way – I was deteriorating. She took hold of my hand and said 'I think a terrible crime has been committed against you Mary. How these people, hiding behind religion, can live without a conscious and do these things to you – they're all criminals!'

It frightened me that I had opened a little of my life to her. I knew I couldn't tell her the full story, but it somehow felt nice to know I had someone who cared, even a little, about me.

She came many more times – each time she visited none of my family saw her – Lyall was out, the older children were at school and the younger ones were having their after-lunch nap. But I had a secret friend! I now worried that Lyall would return and discover I had a friend. Recently Lyall had become even more viscous. Since I wouldn't have anything to do with Tony, Lyall believed I was just there for his sadistic pleasure – and Patricia started to notice the marks on my body left by Lyall's beatings.

Asking what shifts Lyall worked, Patricia avoided Lyall and visited more frequently, and I became even more afraid. After all, now I felt terrible guilt that I had broken the 'code of silence.'

On Patricia's next visit, she told me her idea.

'Now Mary, listen carefully. I believe you could be taught to drive a car.' She shushed my negatives. 'Hear me out … this is very important for your future. You'll never be able to go anywhere with four children – not without transport. You need to learn to drive, and I have a friend who has agreed to teach you.'

'What?' I said in disbelief. Fear began to rise up and I felt faint.

'Listen Mary. Trust me please. I've told my friend you are shy, but he and his wife are good people and want to help. It won't cost you anything to learn to drive. When you have a licence, he will take you to buy a car with the money the doctor is holding for you. It will be in your name.'

I couldn't believe what she was saying. 'I can't…how would I …?' *I can't … I'll never … My God I can't do this … I can't have another secret. Drive a car? I've never even thought … driving … me? How do I keep this from Lyall?* My mind went into a tailspin, but she calmed me down.

'Yes, you can Mary. Trust me. Whilst the big ones are at school, you'll ask a neighbour to mind the small ones and we'll go for a walk up the road. My friends live within walking distance and will meet us, and he'll teach you to drive in their car.'

I felt petrified with fright but, after much persuasion, I gave in. I agreed to go along with this idea … and that's what happened.

They were really nice people, these friends of Patricia. A delightful, pleasant couple, they lived nearby and were happy to be helping me. I slipped away for my lessons, and no-one seemed to notice and soon I learned the basics of driving a car. I eventually passed my driver's test – it wasn't as thorough as tests are today – and accompanied by the couple, I bought an Austin car, in my name, with the money the doctor had held for me. We kept the car parked at their place so that my neighbours or Lyall wouldn't see it.

But now I really had even more secrets from Lyall – a car and a licence to drive it – something I had never imagined I'd ever have. I was so used to being told I was stupid and useless. Good things were happening for me but, inside, I didn't feel any better. I lived in a state of agitation, expecting my secrets to be found out any moment and for me to be punished with a beating.

During this period Patricia and I nearly came undone – it was on a weekday when the convent school had a religious day without students. The four children were at home, so Patricia and I took them for an ice-cream in the car. I became quite nervous about this and told them 'Daddy doesn't need to be told.' *It'll be alright* I told myself, but it wasn't all right because an excited little Michele, in all innocence, told Lyall that my friend had come and bought them ice-creams and I had driven Patricia's car.

Well … the wrath of hell came down on me as Lyall, not for the first time, slammed my head against a wall yelling that I shouldn't have let anyone in.

'You had a secret and now you're in serious trouble.'

Yes, I have a secret … more than one. Heaven help me if you ever find out it's my car and driver's licence, I thought.

Lyall had becoming more and more scary. I never knew when he would come home – I didn't know where he went or where he slept most of the time, but I knew I needed to do something. I saw he was nervous – a sign that he must owe a heap of money to people for his gambling debts. He was missing Tony's regular money and began to take it out on me because I wouldn't have Tony visit. The threats became more physically aggressive and even more abusive.

'You change your mind about Tony,' he'd say menacingly. 'He pays for you. You belong to him, not me.' When I didn't answer, he would push me violently and, because the rooms were empty, there was nothing to stop me crashing into the walls.

He'd shout, 'Perhaps you'd prefer that idiot guy who gave you the kid. Him and his sister are mad in the head. Perhaps you'd like me to bring him round here and give you another idiot kid to care for. You gotta' make changes.'

One day Lyall arrived home with a man and called me into the room saying to him, 'Well, there she is.'

The man said 'Hello.'

Bewildered, I answered, 'Hello.'

Nodding in my direction, Lyall said, 'That's the merchandise. I quoted you a fair price for an hour or two. How long do you want?'

The man said, 'Ask her.'

Lyall laughed and said, 'Phew … don't ask her' and told me to get out the room. The pair went away and that night, when Lyall returned, I had just put the children to bed. He again complained that I hadn't changed my mind about Tony.

I answered, 'I don't want to.'

Lyall screwed up his face in anger. 'Since when do you think you can tell me what you want? You'll do as your told. If you don't do what you're told, I'll get in touch with Ralph. Your father and I are good friends and good money was exchanged for you. He'll make sure you do what you're told.'

I didn't answer, so he shouted furiously, pointing to the children's bedroom. 'You've got three brats in there. Remember … anything can happen.'

The thought of my father's cruelty made me shudder, but I didn't answer so he shouted, 'Yes, or no? I'll count to five.'

He grabbed me by the hair, slamming my head and skinny

frail body against the wall, breaking the fibro. With an enormous bang, the fibro gave way and broke apart, showering dust onto the floor. The noise woke my eldest son, who sleepily came out of his bedroom to see what had happened.

To soothe him Lyall said smoothly, 'She slipped … lucky Daddy was here, eh?' To me he said 'Clean up the mess. I'll give you a couple of days to come to your senses.'

Blood dripped down my face but all I did was clear up the dust and broken fibro pieces on the floor. I should have fought back but deep down I knew I belonged to the Buchanans. They had total control of me.

Lyall's parting words were menacing. 'You're gonna get tired of this before I will.'

Next morning the side of my face looked swollen black and blue, and my eye looked a mess. Pain radiated through my body. Patricia and I had previously arranged for a sign that the coast was clear for her to visit … I would place bits of paper in the window when Lyall wasn't home, and it was safe to call in… but not today. I couldn't talk today.

I felt scared … *Patricia will want to call the police, but they'll take the children away – maybe even take me away* … and it was time for my eldest boy to catch the bus to school. After he'd gone, I didn't put out the sign for Patricia. I became nervous and couldn't think straight. *She'll call the police … I'll be in trouble.* Frantic with worry, when I heard a knock at the door. I half-opened the door to find my next-door neighbour asking after my health.

'Oh Mary, I saw Lyall go out, so I thought I'd check on you. I heard that almighty bang last night. It sounded like a bullet going off. Oh my God, what has he done to your face?'

I shrugged and muttered 'I slipped.'

She didn't believe me and said, 'Is that what that mongrel of a husband did? Are you alright?'

I nodded and she continued 'Can I give you a bit of advice? When they do it once, they do it again and it becomes a habit.

You're married to a mongrel. You need help – what about that blonde lady that comes here?'

I didn't want to have to explain and said, 'She's a friend.'

'Tell her to help you, Mary. God, it looks like you need it.'

Exasperated, she sighed and continued slowly, 'Well Mary, I'll let you into a secret. Most people round here are worried about you. That Flo Lincoln, your mother's friend – she lives in this street, and she's told everyone your mother took her on an expensive holiday – they all think she should have taken you. Your mother needs to look after you. If you need to hide, come in. I'll shelter you … and I won't gossip.'

I thanked her but we both knew I wouldn't be asking for her help.

* * *

I didn't know if this dreadful situation would continue. I felt helpless, anxious, and depressed. I needed some comfort, so I put out the sign for Patricia. When she knocked at the door, secretly I felt pleased. Patricia had passed the house and saw the paper sign, so she came to visit with gifts. She had been knitting and made some beautiful cardigans for the little ones. When she saw the bruising on my eye and the side of my head, she asked what had happened. I couldn't … wouldn't … tell her, but she knew Lyall was bashing me.

'Mary, he's killing you slowly. I believe if he keeps this up there'll be a murder … yours.'

I agreed - there seemed no way that I knew to stop this happening. - *the family will 'get' me one way or another - Mrs Buchanan will destroy me and my children.* I just shrugged and told Patricia I hoped things would get better.

Patricia shook her head. 'He won't get better. Lyall's not going to improve. You must tell me – what happens when he comes home?'

I shrugged. 'Sometimes he sits out there on the steps. He has bits of paper which he writes on, then puts them in his bag.'

'What about food?'

'Sometimes he brings some home and I cook it for him.'

'What about you and the children?'

'No … that's his food. I have to find the food for us.'

Patricia seemed horrified and started to tell me how things should, could, change. I listened but I didn't really take any of it in. However, something inside me gave me hope. Patricia talked about a future which sounded so good … but I felt too scared to make a move. She kept asking me questions and I so wanted to tell her - the secrets were getting too hard to keep. When she found we had no food in the house, she insisted on giving me money to buy food which, she told me, I had to hide it so Lyall wouldn't find and ask questions. When she left, Patricia looked shocked. Perhaps she wondered if she'd ever see me alive again.

That night, Lyall returned and continued ranting at me. 'You're still putting on this act about Tony?' Don't you go getting smart and have that dame come here. You 'd better tell her I'm the boss. Don't you try to change anything - I've got plans.'

I didn't want to think about any frightening changes he had in mind but a few days later, when he came home whistling, I hoped things would settle down. The following day was Saturday and Lyall left for work, arriving back a short time later, accompanied by Mrs Buchanan, daughter Joyce and her two little girls.

I was sitting on the steps with Michele in the backyard, watching the boys playing. Hearing footsteps, I turned, and my heart sank when I saw them all standing in the house. *What do they want - they've never been here before?*

We all said 'Hello' and Lyall announced, 'Mum's got something to say to you and you'd better listen.'

Mrs Buchanan stood tall, looking down at me, sitting on the steps, and said 'I'm going to take Michele to live with us. She's Lyall's child, not yours.'

Did I hear right? What's she saying? I said, 'What?'

Lyall hollered 'Don't say 'What'.'

Mrs Buchanan continued. 'I've come to take her back with us. She'll have a bed and everything. She's better off with us. Look at you all – sleeping on the floor.'

Joyce interrupted, saying soothingly to me, 'She'll be all right – she'll have her own bed and she'll be fine.'

Mrs Buchanan looked at Michele and said 'You want to sleep in a bed, don't you? Daddy wants you to come live with us - Joyce, and the little girls and Nannie.'

Michele was almost nine years old. She stood cowering behind me and asked in a trembling whisper, 'Do I have to go?'

Mrs Buchanan looked at Lyall 'Tell her Lyall. Tell her why.'

He spoke slowly to Michele. 'Do you know what a five-pound note is?'

She nodded.

'Do you get any money off your Mum?'

She shook her head.

'Well … I can give you five-pound of your own to spend.'

Michele shook her head and began to look anxious. She started to tear up and clung to me and the boys had stopped playing and were watching - listening. They began to look scared too. With the children watching, looking fearful, Mrs Buchanan turned abruptly and walked back into the house, followed by Joyce, her children, and Lyall.

'I don't want to go Mummy,' Michele mumbled into my hair as she cuddled into me.

'You don't have to go darling.' *She loves me and wants to be with me* I thought happily. 'Don't get upset. I'll tell her. Nothing will happen to you.'

Joyce came back and chipped in. 'You're not making it any easier Mary.'

'I don't want to make it easier' I said.

'Mumma always told you she was Lyall's,' Joyce repeated softly. 'She wants to go.'

'She doesn't want to,' I replied, terrified at what was happening – *this is my worst nightmare, something I've dreaded ever since her birth. She'd always said Michele was hers – a Buchanan.*

Mrs Buchanan obviously wanted this to be over. 'Come on' she barked out, and soon I heard the front door close shut behind them all.

Lyall glared at me as I said, 'She wants to be with me not her.'

Michele looked up at me and said, 'What about the money?'

I sighed and my stomach turned somersaults as I said. 'I can't give you any money.'

In my heart I knew I had no control … she was Lyall's baby. Michele had a disturbed night and the next day Lyall started again, saying to Michele 'Have you ever seen a five-pound note? I'm going to give you a five-pound note, and you can buy whatever you like.'

Wide-eyed, Michele said nothing, but she listened.

I heard Lyall's cajoling voice. 'With a five-pound note, you can buy toys or sweeties - whatever you want.'

Michele nodded, thought for a while then announced, 'I'm going to go with Nannie.'

I felt shattered and said, 'I thought you wanted to live with me – I thought you liked going to school and meeting your friends.'

My daughter looked at me and said, 'I do like going to school …but with Nannie I can have things.'

'You can have things here' I murmured with a broken heart.

'No, not like that.

'You don't want to go,' I implored. 'You said so.'

'I do now' she replied. 'If I get that money, I can buy everything I want, and she said I don't have to sleep on the floor.'

The Buchanans came for her again. They trooped in and Mrs Buchanan looked at Michele and said, 'Show Nannie where your things are.' She took Michele's hand and went to the bedroom.

I must have looked as though I would cry. 'Now, don't think you can go making a fuss – you'll do as you're told,' Lyall ordered, glaring at me with a threatening expression, as I sat stunned, unable to think how to stop them taking my daughter. They returned with Mrs Buchanan carrying a bundle of clothes. I looked at Michele and pleaded 'You told me you didn't want to go.'

Michele looked at me innocently and said, 'I can stay with Nannie. Nannie says I'm a big girl now. I still love you.'

Joyce interrupted, looking at Lyall, '… and Daddy loves you too …' He kept quiet but grinned triumphantly. Gently pressing Michele towards me, Joyce said, 'Give her a kiss and tell her you'll be seeing her soon.'

I sat glued to my seat. I couldn't think, couldn't say anything. *No … no…. It can't be happening.*

Michele gave me a kiss on the cheek. Somehow I knew this would be my last. It was the most tortuous moment of my life.

'Now, give me your hand darling,' Joyce said. She looked at me and whispered, 'I'll make sure she knows you love her' … and they were gone.

With a breaking heart, I looked out the window and saw them sitting in their car outside. I felt like someone had cut off my arm. The boys asked me where Michele was going but I couldn't tell them …I just said. 'They've got a bed for her.'

I continued to stare out the window - *my little girl – she's gone – and all for a five-pound note.* Patricia called in later saying she felt anxious about me. When she saw my expression and slumped shoulders, she asked 'What's happened?'

I told her and she said, 'I'll call the police. They'll get her back.'

I shook my head. 'No, they might take the boys too.'

'Oh Mary … you look so unwell. Have you eaten?'

'No there's no food.'

'What, nothing?'

'No he's never even wanted to feed the little girl who looks like him, never mind me and the boys. 'The black bastards' is what the Buchanan family call the boys.'

She pleaded with me – 'well … leave. Just leave.'

I shook my head.

Where will I go? Apart from you I have no one. At least here I have a roof over my head.

This all seemed too much for Patricia – overwhelmed, she burst into tears. When I asked her why, she said she was sobbing for me and the children. 'This is the cruellest act I've ever heard of – I feel ill. Look I just popped in because I was worried about you. I've brought some food; you must eat, you're not well. Please put the sign out if he's not here. You mustn't keep anything from me.'

After she left, I was in a daze. For the first time, my brain slowly started to whirl. *She's the only person who thinks we have a future. If I had gone with her when she first suggested it, we wouldn't have been here, and they couldn't have taken Michele.*

The next day, on our way to the doctor for his last appointment, my son asked when Michele was coming back. I replied I didn't know - she was with Nannie. I felt so ill, everything ached, and I saw, from the reflection in the bathroom mirror, my face had swollen up.

When he saw me, Dr Egan asked what happened to my face and I told him I'd slipped.

'I don't believe that of course, but you're obviously not going to tell me. Are you doing something about it?'

I shook my head but on my way home, I kept hearing, in my mind, what Patricia had said.

'Are you ever going to do something about the situation Mary?'

I had shrugged, but Patricia had continued…'I really hope so … I know the truth – no-one told me but it's obvious there's bad things going on in your life. You can't keep it up.'

I walked home with a heavy heart. I missed Michele but I knew I had to decide. I never made decisions before but now I have to. *If I don't agree to having Tony back, he'll bring someone else home. What shall I do?*

That night I woke up with Lyall's hand over my mouth. 'Now shut up. You're going to have Tony back, d'ya hear? You've been a bit of a smart arse and I don't like it. If I tell Ralph, he won't like it either. He'll put you somewhere else where you definitely won't like.'

I nodded and said nothing. His threats were becoming increasingly alarming. Just when I thought things couldn't get any worse, it did. I couldn't risk Patricia coming to the house. I felt too frightened to make a decision and also, I worried that Lyall might catch her. Things were spinning out of control, and I was missing Michele. I asked Lyall when I could see her. He replied, 'When you start doing as you're told.'

'She's MY girl…my girl,' I pleaded.

'Don't start this again …when you start seeing Tony' was his reply. 'When you do as you're told I might let you see her.'

'She's my girl' was all I could reply.

'Don't you have enough to do with the others? He said, indicating the boys.

'You said I'd see her again,' I muttered.

'I said 'might' – 'might' means when you do what I say.'

I couldn't stop myself, but I wasn't going to give in to him. 'But I want to see Michele – it's what I want.'

He looked really irritated now as he shouted 'I know what you want but I never promised to do anything. Just shut up and do as you're told.'

What should I do? I so want to see Michele, but … I won't … I don't want to see Tony … ever again.

Things changed again. Overnight, Lyall told me to get in the room and sleep with the boys. Then I heard a woman's voice and her footsteps as they went into a bedroom. This happened on three occasions, and I knew they were different women each night – their voices and the sound of their shoes when they walked, their footsteps were different. I realised these were women who didn't have the money to pay their fare. Now they didn't 'do it' in the taxi anymore – he brought them into our house. I listened as he boasted that, if they ever wanted to gamble, to let him know and he would take them to his mother's. I smiled to myself. *What these women would want with a night of gambling, I don't know - they can't even pay their taxi fare. It surely isn't his good looks that brought them to our home.*

Then once, during the day, he brought a woman home, but he

must have had another job to do and told me 'I'll be gone for a short while – about forty minutes. I'm leaving her here – be nice … and keep your mouth shut. I'll be back.'

When he left, she glared at me and said, 'Do you know how to make a cup of tea?' She stared hard and repeated, 'I want a cup of tea.' I shrugged and she ordered 'Well, make me one.'

I didn't move - just stood staring back at her and she warned me. 'Look, I'll tell Lyall. You work for him, and I want a cup of tea.'

I nodded and went to see if we had any tea. She followed me into the kitchen as I boiled the water.

'We don't have any milk' I said, 'There's no refrigerator.'

'Yes – I can see that. You got all his furniture sent away, didn't you?'

I didn't answer but said 'Do you want sugar?'

'Make it a teaspoonful,' she said. She was standing behind me and continued, 'Why don't you piss off? You work for him, but he doesn't like you. Where are you from?'

'From? I asked.

'From? … which country.?'

'From here' I replied.

'Lyall says you come from India. I don't know why you don't just go - piss off.'

A short while later, Lyall returned and said to the woman 'Has she been talking?'

She looked hard at me and replied, 'I asked for a cup of tea, and she made me one. I had to have it without milk since you have no fridge.'

He looked hard at me then took her into another room and twenty minutes later they both left.

* * *

A few days later there was a knock on the door and when I opened it, there stood my mother, dressed smartly and beautifully presented. Surprised, wondering why she was visiting, I let her in and took her into the lounge.

'Do you expect me to sit on that old chair,' she snapped, looking around at the empty room. 'What a mess you've made of all this.'

I wanted to say it wasn't me that made a mess of things, it was Lyall and his gambling- but I wasn't used to answering back so I didn't – but for the very first time, I thought it.

'Come outside and see my nice new car' she said gaily, and I followed her outside where she proceeded to show it to me, before getting in and driving off.

Dispirited, I went back into the house. *Not a word about the children or ask how I was*, I thought. *Why did she come ... not a word!*

A few moments later, my sweet neighbour came and knocked on the door. I let her in, and we sat on the worn chairs.

'I couldn't help but see your mother had visited. Did she give you anything?'

I shook my head.

'Did she offer you anything?'

Again I shook my head.

My neighbour became quite upset. 'Doesn't she see your need? Doesn't she make a fuss of you? She obviously has enough money to help you.'

Once again, I shook my head and shrugged. So she told me about her own mother. 'My mother is very class conscious. She thinks I married beneath me, living here in a Housing Commission home, but if I asked for help, she'd give it to me ... because I'm her child. That's what parents do, even when their children grow up. They love their children even as adults.'

This was a new idea to me. She asked where Michele was as she hadn't seen her for a few days, and I explained she was staying with her Nannie. I told her I missed her and so wanted to see her, and Lyall had said he might let me see her soon.

'My God, why *might* he let you see her?

I just stared back at her. *What could I tell her that would make her understand without breaking the 'code of silence'?*
'You don't have to take it Mary,' she said solemnly.

But, for the moment, I knew that I had to. Before she left, she offered to take me to a doctor, but I shook my head and realised I must look pretty bad.

After she'd gone, I looked up the street and saw my mother talking to her friend, Mrs Lincoln. They were looking at the new car, then said their good-byes and my mother drove off. I returned inside and sat on the chair – to think.

My neighbour's mother didn't agree with her marriage, but she would still be kind to her if she needed her. Am I so different to anyone else? I've always done what I'm told. I look after the little boys, keep them clean and make the food go round. Why doesn't my mother like me? She's never, ever said she loved me.

I'd never, ever thought these things out before, but I had no answers. I'd read somewhere that children wanted love, so I'd tried to make my children feel special and wanted. I didn't know what I'd done wrong, but I had never felt loved. I did know however, that I didn't feel well. I knew something was wrong with me and my mother didn't even notice.

Now you readers will be thinking *why the heck didn't she just leave?* Looking back I know I should have said *I'm going to get Michele back and leave with the boys* but, in those days, I didn't think for myself – I thought like a slave – it had been in-bred in me. I just did as I was told.

I didn't put the sign out for Patricia, but she came anyway as she was worried. When she saw me, she became even more worried … 'I'm getting more and more frightened for you, Mary, you look so ill … so thin. Have you seen Michele yet?'

I shook my head and, without thinking, I repeated Lyall's threat, 'If I behave, he might let me.'

Patricia studied me with a shocked expression as she said 'What does he mean by that? The children are fine, and the place is clean.

What else does he want?' Then she stared hard and said 'Oh God Mary, I can see new marks on your throat and your head looks bruised. Mary you're not eating, I can see you don't look good.'

I said nothing and she continued 'What does he mean Mary? You're not telling me everything.'

I blurted out 'He brought a woman home.'

'What sort of woman?'

'She told me to piss off. She asked me if I came from India. That's what Lyall told her – I came from India.'

Patricia's face turned red. 'He's an animal and so are his family – and they have your little girl.'

'I do miss her.'

'He's not going to let you see Michele. He'll hold it over you and the children.' She gave a gasp of exasperation. 'I don't understand any of this and I know you won't tell me anymore but Mary, there's a whole world out there. Just leave.'

I told her how my mother had been in the house for a few minutes then visited a neighbour with her new car and about the conversation with my neighbour. Patricia's eyes filled with tears. 'I could cry for you. If I go to the police, I could stop all this. These people have committed so many offenses against you. I can't let them get away with it or I too will be party to the crimes. Mary, you have rights - for your children and in marriage. Mary, you are a person, a person with rights – not a slave to your husband or anyone else.'

'Oh … but I am.'

'No you're not. You're a young woman who's never been taught your rights by your family. I know my rights because my family taught me. You haven't been out there, but you have to think about it for your own sake and for your children.' She shuddered and continued 'I think about you all the time. Your eyes never smile except when you look at your children with love … and Mary, you have many reasons to smile.'

I sensed her sympathy and remembered she had been such a

gentle girl at school. *She never had a loud voice back then, not even in the playground. She's made choices. She's free like a butterfly, even after leaving her bullying husband.*

Patricia looked at me with a serious face and said 'I'll come back in two days' time – don't worry. I won't come in if he's here. He's using Michele as a weapon. She's safe and they'll keep her happy, so, of course, she wants to stay with them. It's time we got you and the boys out of this house to make you safe too.'

She took my hand and said 'You're a licensed driver with a car. We have a way to get you and the boys away. Now don't look away Mary.' Her eyes bored into my face as she repeated 'You're not a slave. If you refuse, you're putting your life and the boys in danger. Michele is not in jeopardy, but you are. Be brave Mary, be strong. You're a person. You can be free, think about it and I will come again. Think about a future Mary – whilst you still have one.'

* * *

When Lyall came home the next day, he glared at me and said 'I'm getting in touch with Tony. He's gonna come back here if you want to see the girl. You're gonna do as you're told.'

I didn't look him in the eye, and he must have suspected my nervousness, so he persisted, quizzing me. 'I'm asking you now, has that girl, that other one – you know who I mean – has she been here?'

I shook my head and said 'No,' avoiding his eyes, and for the very first time I didn't feel guilty at telling a lie.

Lyall glared at me. 'Remember, you belong to me, and you do exactly what I say. Any nonsense and I'll tell Ralph and you know what he'll do. Don't you remember what happened to Linda Agostini?'

The name meant nothing to me, and I said so.

'You're so dumb and stupid. Course you know her' Lyall replied. 'Don't act dumb. Your family knew her – your mother thought she was her sister and she ended up dead. Just you remember what happened to Linda. Do as you're told, or I'll tell Ralph. I'll let Tony know you're ready. He'll come in a couple of days, and he'll want his moneys-worth so shut up and do as I tell you.'

I didn't argue but, actually, I did remember the case of 'The Pyjama Girl' – Linda Agostini. My mother had gone to check the dead girl in case it was Mary, her missing older sister – but it wasn't.

Next day all I could think about was that Lyall obviously owed a lot of money. These people could kill me and the children, but I didn't want to put the paper sign out for Patricia. I was frightened and not used to making decisions. I didn't know what I was going to tell Patricia next time she came - but come she did.

'Are you going to come with me Mary?' she asked straight away.

'I think so,' I replied with a sigh, my heart thumping in my chest.

Patricia looked at me and shook her head. 'No, no …I don't want you to 'think,' she said gently.

Trembling with anxiety. I said, 'I don't know what to do.' I felt dizzy and thought my legs might give way.

'I'll tell you – get your things and get the children's' things.'

I was a bag of nerves, my mind in a daze. 'But … um … I can't – what do I do?' I mumbled.

'Do you have a suitcase?'

I shrugged and she continued 'Sheets, pillow- cases?'

I said, 'Yes' but I looked hesitant.

Patricia took my hand and said 'I won't be coming here again if you don't come now, Mary. I don't want to find your dead body on the floor. I won't come back to find you and the boys dead.' Hesitant, I stared at her silently, and she continued 'Don't make me go away now. I can take you out into the real world.'

I looked into her face, saw her honesty, and gave In – I nodded. We filled two pillowcases with the children's clothes. I only had a few clothes so everything we owned filled just three pillowcases.

Patricia asked, 'Is there anything in the house that's yours?'
'Nothing.'

She took my hand and touched the wedding ring on my finger, saying 'That might make a little money.'

At the door, she told me she had a plan. We were to take the boys and walk down the street to my car – as though we were going for a walk, in case the neighbours saw us. We'd fold the pram and put it, and the children, into the car then drive back. I'd park nearby and Patricia would take my key, go into the house, and pick up the pillowcases and return to the car to stack them in the boot. She would then get into the car, and I'd drive us all away. Patricia gave me strict instructions.

'... and another thing, keep a low profile and keep your face away from anyone who might be looking.'

I felt stiff with fright as we acted out her plan. There didn't seem to be any neighbours watching us. Patricia climbed into the passenger seat, saying 'Now drive steadily. Don't look up but, when you can, pull over and park.'

I did as she suggested and stopped the car at the top of the street. Patricia said, 'now count to ten.'

I did as she said, slowly counting out loud.

She gazed at me and smiled 'You've just got out of prison Mary. You've done it. You're free, love.'

* * *

CHAPTER 4

THE APPEARANCE OF FREEDOM

For the next half-hour, we drove along with Patricia directing me where to go. With the baby in between them, the two boys were happy in the back seat. Patricia would turn round and talk to the boys from time to time, and my eldest boy asked where we were going.

'Somewhere nice,' she told him, over my shoulder.

To me this was our first day of liberty – freedom from cruelty. I saw people walking in the streets and knew, unlike them, I looked gaunt and thin, and reality dropped in. *People won't want to know me – they don't know my secrets. Anyway, I'm just another woman. Oh gosh! What have I done? How will I live?*

'I have to pull over,' I muttered and stopped the car at the side of the road as Patricia asked what was wrong.

Scared, I stared at her and murmured, 'How will I cope Patricia? I might look like everyone else on the outside but inside I'm not.'

'But you are …' she insisted.

'Patricia, I don't know how to live. I only smile when I'm told to – how can I live like them without instructions?'

She reached across and took my hand. 'You are an intelligent woman, Mary. See how quickly you learned to drive, and you drive so well. A while ago you never thought you could ever do that – now you are going to live your own life, free from your family, and you CAN do that too.'

I wasn't convinced and felt quite sad when I thought about my children being uprooted.

'… and little Michele won't be with us.'

'Mary, she's safe. They'll do nice things to keep her happy and make her want to stay. She's safe … but you wouldn't have been if you had stayed. I don't know about Lyall's mental state, but I think it's getting worse - you had to leave.'

Becoming calmer I asked, 'Where am I driving to?'

'We're going to someone's house. They are a nice older couple whose adult children have moved away. I've told them all about you and the boys.'

I must have appeared uncomfortable, and she continued 'Not your secrets Mary, but I've known them for years and they will take care of you.'

My stomach started churning as I thought back to Lyall. 'What's gonna happen when Lyall finds I've gone?'

Patricia shrugged, 'well, he can't go to the police.'

'He might tell my family though,' I replied quickly.

Patricia's voice was unruffled as she leaned towards me and countered, 'And are they going to go to the police? They'd be asked why you left home – and with three children. Your family can't get involved with the authorities. There'd be too many questions to answer.'

I shuddered and whispered, 'They'll find me.'

'Mary,' Patricia soothingly replied, 'they don't know where you are, and they don't know me, and if they go to the police, there'd be too many questions asked and they'd be in a lot of trouble. Now stop worrying, start the car and we'll go on.'

But they'll find me, I thought.

* * *

I didn't know that Patricia had already arranged for us to stay with her friends – for anonymity I'll call them Betty and Bob. By the time we arrived at their brick house, in the western suburbs of Sydney, the children were tired and hungry, and I was visibly shaking. Betty and Bob were a welcoming couple; they ushered us inside and offered a cup of tea. My nerves were shattered, and I swayed as I walked into the house but inside it was a warm and comfortable feeling – like putting on a pair of warm, fluffy slippers. Patricia knew her way round and she put the kettle on.

Recalling this makes me cry now – it brings me to tears as I think back. So now I cry for Mary, the little girls, and the little boys – I'm alive and my children are safe, but I cry for Mary who couldn't open up to Patricia. Of course I had told her a little of my dreadful life but not the deep horror of it. I tried to put on a brave face as they talked about going to doctors. I became even more terrified as I thought how I would be traced by my family. I couldn't see I'd been set free – I didn't know the full meaning of independence. I didn't pause to take in the future plans that were being suggested – where I would live with the children, schools, go to see doctors. All that was blocked out – what was going through my mind was what my family would do – what my father Ralph, my mother and the Buchanans would do when they found I'd walked away. *They'll have people out searching for us. I'll suffer for this. They won't let me go.*

Whilst I was happy to be amongst friendly people, I was completely terrified – certain that my family would get me back and punish me, maybe even make trouble for Patricia, Betty, and Bob. I didn't know any different and I was really in shock. I walked, talked, and smiled but I had no ideas of my own, only Patricia's ideas. How could I tell her that I was shivering with fear inside?

Reader, please try and understand that I talk about this in truth – put yourself in my shoes and understand me. I cry now for the tears I couldn't cry then. From early childhood, I became good at suppressing or even showing my feelings, for fear of receiving even more punishment than everyone gave me. Now I know it's called disassociation – my mind removed me from what was actually happening.

Rescued from those horrors, I understood I'd been tossed and tumbled into a new world of thinking. *I've always been told I'm stupid ... ignorant ... of no value. I don't know if I CAN think for myself.*

We sat at a table and these wonderful people put food on the plates. As we talked, I began to feel that, despite my missing her, Michele would be alright. Speaking of my fears, Betty said she was sure the Buchanans would look after her - but not to expect them to tell her I'd been a wonderful mother.

'They'll just care for her ... so she's safe.'

I soon saw that Patricia had done her homework as she set out a well-thought-out plan for me to see doctors.

'Mary, there are many things we can do to help you – and you will need help. How would you feel if Betty was to mind the children whilst we take you for appointments with doctors?'

'If I do this, will I be able to work? To get a job?'

'Yes Mary, of course. You'll be able to work and provide for the children.'

I was torn. I feared a future of retribution - where Mrs Buchanan would say it was all my fault. Everything would be blamed on me - it normally was - and I wasn't used to thinking. One thing I did know though, was that I was sick – I felt so ill – there was so much pain - but I wasn't sure about going to a doctor or hospital where they might discover my earlier history of abuse. I hadn't fully opened up to Patricia and things might come out about my past that I didn't want to discuss or even remember.

I agreed but I wasn't enthusiastic. I wanted to feel better, to feel strong but it all seemed so overwhelming, the thought of having to see doctors. *They'll see what I've been covering up and it'll be even more questions I don't want to answer.*

When Patricia suggested we walk outside for some fresh air

and exercise I shrugged it off. I dreaded leaving the house, but she persuaded me that we could do it in the evening – just little walks when few people were around. I didn't understand the concept of doing things for pleasure and exercising. She finally persuaded me to walk with her, but I was terrified as I watched every shadow and held onto her arm. I felt terribly anxious.

I quickly realised that I couldn't stop being afraid just because I had been set free from the family. I hadn't told Patricia but, each time we walked outside, I expected someone to jump out the shadows and attack us. My nerves were stretched taut. I wasn't expecting a family member to accost us. I don't know about Lyall, he just took orders from his mother, but people like my father and the Buchanans didn't do their own dirty work; they had others do the deed for them. I couldn't see that the Buchanans or my family would just let me get away or Lyall, who was losing his money-spinner. He had no love for me – or for that matter, his mother nor anyone else – but money had changed hands and he would want me back. These weren't the sort of people to let anyone get away with anything. I felt certain he would complain to my father. Their associates were people from the dark side of the criminal world, who fixed things for them, and I knew my brothers, whilst not professional criminals, would do my father's bidding. I feared they, or someone, would be out there – waiting to catch me.

I had this fear embedded in me and neither Patricia nor her friends could begin to understand the guilt and shame I felt. I appreciated these friends took a tremendous risk to care for me and the boys, but I knew they could never understand my fears. Unlike my relations, they would never hurt a living soul and they deserved protection from my family. The boys seemed happy, but I was rigid with fear most of the time. So, when I went to sleep each night, my mind was filled with fear - not as content as I was pretending to be.

It was bad of me, but I hadn't told Patricia that we were all in danger. I was too panicky to tell her how worried I was, knowing my family and what they would do to get me back. *I'm an earning commodity to the family, and I've put Patricia, Betty, and Bob, in danger. Betty and Bob are two of the kindest people, and in their loving goodness, want to help me and my little boys. Patricia told them what she knew about my life, but I haven't told her the entire story. I've kept my darkest secrets hidden. Most of what she knows is that I have an abusive husband, and my family were indifferent to my terrible situation.*

I should have been more honest, but I had to be who I was then. Fearful of retribution, embarrassment and the 'code of silence' stopped me telling anymore and horrifying Patricia. Each day Patricia and Betty showed me how to live and love, and I gradually learned to do things. In the most loving way, the boys were taken out of my hands and Patricia's plans were activated. She made all the arrangements for my eldest boy, to go to school and keep the other two fed and happy.

My heart kept telling me this was too good to be true. It was hard for me not to be excited and jump out of bed every day – I learned so many different things. Patricia taught me I wasn't her slave, I wasn't anybody's slave, but it was hard to comprehend after a lifetime of total brainwashing, fear and taking orders. Betty made me soups, but I couldn't eat much. My sleeping pattern was awful -nightmares and tossing and turning all night - and I suffered from many medical ailments - troubles that had gone undetected over the years. Patricia picked up on this and told me I urgently needed to see a doctor.

'Mary you must eat, and I'm going to take you to a doctor soon. Your life has taken its toll, but you cannot go on not eating. Something will happen to you, and we don't want that. Think about your children … I know you will agree.'

I was aware I looked like a skeleton with skin. From my reflection, I saw my skin seemed to be stretched so tight it was almost see-through. Every day was full of pain and each muscle in my body ached - I felt so tired. I wanted to feel better, and I also knew my children needed their mother, so I nodded in agreement.

'You may just need a tonic,' she muttered without meeting my eyes. I knew neither of us believed this.

We were living in Leichhardt, known for its very European population, mainly Italian. Patricia took me on a walk round the block on a number of occasions ... not to the big shops, just the residential area. She wanted me to feel life, to feel free. She'd suggested I look at people, look at their gardens and the flowers. Each time we went out she took me for a walk and told me she wanted me to go out walking independently, on my own - to look in the shops, to feel unrestricted, to do what I wanted, not to feel accountable - but she didn't understand that I couldn't just go out and feel at ease.

Living with Lyall, I had gone to the local shops and bought food there; I had gone to the local chemist and the doctor, but apart from going to the hospital – or my mother's, or even Tony's house - I did not go out unless there was a reason to go, and then I returned as fast as I could. I wasn't used to walking for pleasure or being out on my own. I suffered from agoraphobia and needed to have something to hold on to, a wall or a railing, in case I lost my balance or had a panic attack - there was always fear and worry. I could never relax – my nerves were stretched tight, and I felt very brittle.

One sunny day, Patricia had gone to work, and Betty encouraged me to get outside in the sunshine.

'It's a beautiful day out there.'

It took all my courage, but I went out for a short walk, and it seemed nice to walk the footpath – people passed and sometimes nodded socially. This was all new to me. A little scared, I returned, and Betty said 'You didn't go far; you were only away a short time. Go out again and walk to the shops and have a look around. You have money in your pocket. If you get lost, you can stop a taxi. With the money you can pay for the taxi to bring you back to this address.'

'Mmm ... maybe next time,' I replied.

So, gradually I began to think I should try again. A few days later I decided I would … I would go to the shops. I thought *OK… OK… what will I do if I get lost? Yes, I do know. I'll get a taxi back here.* Armed with money and the address, out I went and walked to a main road but left quickly, returning home to Betty. Again I'd lost my nerve.

Betty was very thoughtful. 'When you get really adventurous you should buy a cup of coffee there at the shops' she advised and a few days later encouraged me again. I had money in a little purse and recalled her idea – *if I become lost or nervous, I can always hail a taxi to bring me back.*

That day, nerves on edge, I walked to the shopping area - to a big intersection on the outside of the shopping centre. There were people everywhere and it felt very strange. Within a few minutes, a man came up to me and asked me how I was. I looked around to see if he was really talking to me … he was. I didn't know him. Frightened, I nodded and backed away – my heart in my mouth.

'I'm alright,' I mumbled. I wasn't very smart then – certainly not smart enough to just walk on.

He spoke soothingly, but in a dominating voice. 'I think you should come with me. Come with me - I've got the car round the corner.'

Alarmed, I began to walk away. He must have seen my fear and started to sing out loudly. 'Look at her. Look at her. She left her husband and little children. She's a prostitute – she walked out on her husband and left her children. She's a prostitute.'

Around me, I saw people had stop to stare. Some passing women were eyeing me in disgust. An elderly man joined in, loudly exclaiming, 'Go home to your husband, you prostitute' and the original man continued loudly.

'Yes. You, come home, you come with me now. I'll take you home to your young children. Your poor husband – your poor children.'

Stiff with fright I saw a taxi driving towards us and hailed it. Relieved, I saw it draw near but this man sang out to the driver, 'She's a prostitute - a prostitute,' and the driver sped up and drove away.

Now I was in a terrible panic. Terrified, I wanted to flee from the man, the crowd of women and the shouting. In a panic I turned and hurried blindly across the road; my only thought was to separate myself from this awful scene. Unknowingly I had walked out into the thick traffic; there were cars everywhere. The air filled with sounds of screeching tyres and drivers honking their horns and shouting at me. Oblivious to the chaos and danger, I ran - arriving safely on the opposite pavement. In fear, as I ran, I looked back to see if I was being followed but the first man had run the other way – to get his car, I suppose. I saw people staring after me, scowls on their faces. I hurried on down a side street and kept going, turning corners, my heart beating fast. All I could think was, *this is exactly what I feared; exactly what I knew Lyall, and my family would do – have someone tail me. It actually happened … well, I got away … but they won't give up. They'll keep searching.*

However, I soon realised I was lost so, still frantic with fear, I slowed my walking pace, but continued to turn corners, watching out for a taxi. Thankfully, one came in sight, and I hailed it, giving the driver Betty's address. Told to hop in, I sank back into the seat … safe … but the sound of my heart thumped loudly in my ears. I arrived home and Betty took one look at me and could see I was traumatised. 'What's wrong' she asked?

I stammered out what had happened, and she said, 'I think we both need a cup of tea.'

When Patricia came home, she listened to my tale of upset and dismissed my fears. 'But Mary, nobody knows you're here … nobody. It was a one-in-a-million thing. Did you recognise him … this man who yelled?'

I sat shivering as I replied, 'No … but so many people went to the Buchanan's house for gambling … I took no notice of them - but he must have recognised me.'

'No, no…' Pat repeated firmly, shaking her head. 'nobody knows you're here … it was a one-in-a-million thing - believe me Mary. Now calm down. I'll take the day off work this week. I've found a wonderful doctor and I want to take you to see him. Stop worrying. We won't go out for walks, and no-one knows you're here. You're safe … just keep calm.'

I kept repeating, 'You don't understand. They won't ever let me go.' It plunged me into feeling extreme terror. *What will happen? I've never ever told anyone anything about my life – it's an unspoken rule, but my father will think I've talked, and he knows some real nasty people - he'll use them … I know, he'll use them … on me.* My fear grew and grew inside me – so bad that I could hardly speak.

* * *

CHAPTER 5

LEARNING TO LIVE LIFE

As the date of the doctor's appointment drew nearer, I became more terrified with each waking moment. I still couldn't eat more than a mouthful of food and my sleep was intermittent and full of nightmares. I knew I looked like someone who'd been in a prison-of-war camp – skin and bone; I weighed about six stone (38 Kilos) which was far too light for my five-foot-nine (1.79 metres) body.

The day arrived….

'We have an appointment today Mary,' Patricia said gently, taking my hand..'

'Do I really have to go?' I pleaded. My nerves were on edge and I dreaded leaving the house. Pain was a daily occurrence for me, and I knew a doctor's examination would see how I had been miss-treated and used. I dreaded my secrets being outed for all to see.

I hopped Patricia might shake her head, but she said 'Yes Mary, we're friends and I 've so wanted you out of that house, away from your evil husband. You're ill and I don't want you to die now. Please say you'll come.'

I knew I needed help and gave in with a sigh. 'Yes.'

Patricia seemed relieved and said 'Right, we'll have to leave soon as it's a bit of a drive away.'

Shocked I replied 'Oh, I can't drive there.'

'Oh yes Mary, you can. I'll sit next to you and direct the way. You'll be fine. You drive well.'

Patricia helped me wash my hair with sweet-smelling shampoo and I calmed down as I breathed in the aroma. We talked about what to wear; I had come with few clothes, but Patricia had gathered together a few skirts and blouses for me. I looked presentable but the garments hung on me.

As I drove to see Doctor Stulzman, I became even more aware of being unmasked – playing over and over in my head, the scene at the shops, the man shouting 'she's a prostitute' … *What'll happen when the doctor examines me? What will he find out?* The journey was a difficult drive for me as I became more nervous with each mile.

'I'll be there with you, Mary,' Patricia stated, over and over, to try to calm me. 'I've told him about your background, so you don't have to explain everything to him. You would like me to be there with you when you see Doctor Stulzman, wouldn't you?"

I agreed and that gave me more confidence. *He would only know what Patricia knew and she didn't know the whole truth – and she would be with me … what a relief!*

The doctor was kind and soothing in his manner - it gradually made me feel less anxious. He could see I was frail and undernourished and only asked about my food intake. Patricia must have told him all she knew as he told me he could see in my face how unhappy I was - 'you smile, but your eyes don't smile' and that he had seen similar before – people who had been experienced cruelty and had been in concentration camps. He explained that being so undernourished left me open to many health disorders. He suggested he could help me back to good health, to provide nutrition intravenously, since I was unable to consume food easily.

'We would have to do this for some time Mary. It will allow you to recover your physical health - for yourself and your children, Mary. I understand that you have been physically and mentally beaten but there's a beautiful world out there, waiting for you to learn about it. You will have to come back every second day for the injections for your physical health but, Mary, you also need to learn about the good in life – nobody ordering or telling you what to do or how to think. You have to repair your mental health - there's laughter, music, people, and wonderful things out there. Patricia can help you – I suggest you let her guide you.'

I reluctantly agreed and he administered an intravenous injection and informed me I needed to return in two days for another. Back at the car, exhausted from the mental anguish I'd gone through, I looked at Patricia. I felt drained of energy.

'I don't think I can drive.'

Patricia patiently encouraged me, and we returned home – it had been a big experience for me especially as I'd been dreading seeing a doctor since it was first mentioned … but Patricia had another outing on her mind.

At home she explained. 'On Friday evening we're going out somewhere nice – nice place, nice people, nice music.' She must have seen the look of horror on my face and asked 'Mary, you do like music, don't you?'

I shrugged…*did I like music? I suppose I did.*

'I know a really splendid place near the Harbour Bridge – its run by nice people with coffee and a live band. It has a tiny dance floor where some people like to dance and it's quiet, - it's out of the way and no-one stares it's called 'Malado'. What do you think Mary? Will you come with me?'

I saw Patricia gazing back at me with her innocent eyes and it dissolved my instinct to say 'no.' In my heart I didn't want to go but I knew I had to make an effort and I nodded - agreeing for her sake.

I continued with the intravenous injections and slowly began to eat a mouthful or two of food. When Friday came along, we checked through the clothes Patricia had gathered for me. I had brought nothing but a threadbare dress and a change of underwear with me – all I owned. She chose a long-sleeved pastel frock for me and helped me dress my hair. Betty said we both looked beautiful as we left to make our way to the car.

In the warm early evening, we drove into the city and on to the Harbour Bridge where the traffic became heavy – my pulse was racing, I thought I might die of fright as I drove amongst the aggressive drivers, across the bridge. By now it was dark, and we found parking near the Malado cafe. In the car outside, we sat and watched people going in and I felt myself beginning to shake.

'Come on Mary' Patricia said, and we left the car and walked towards the entrance. I stopped outside – my legs were trembling, and my head swam. We could see inside, through the window, that the lights were low, and people sat at tables, their faces lit by the soft light of a candle on each table. Everyone appeared pleasant enough, but I panicked. *I can't see a door – where's another door?* - and I blurted out 'I can't go in – I can't see a door – a way to get out.'

Patricia calmed me explaining there was another exit at the back and to follow her inside. Ever since my childhood, after being shut in a wardrobe by my parents, I suffered from claustrophobia. It took a great deal of anxiety and faith in Patricia to follow her. I tried to keep my face calm, and didn't look left or right, but followed Patricia's back until we reached a booth. We sat in the gloom of the candle-light room, listening to the band playing 'Bechome Mucho.' I loved the soothing music – so soft and gentle – and very slowly my terror subsided, and for a few moments, I almost felt safe.

Patricia ordered coffee and suggested I look around, so, feeling brave, I did. I saw a few couples, one table with a lot of young men chatting and laughing, and a few men sitting on their own. The sweet gentle music was provided by a trio and Patricia told me how much she liked it here - she often came after work. 'It's just a nice peaceful place where you can relax ... and Mary, no-one recognises you and you don't know anyone either.'

We sipped our coffee and listened to the music and gradually my shaking subsided. I sensed myself relaxing. This was my first night out. I knew I would always remember it.

* * *

I continued to have the intravenous injections and I had to admit, they did make me feel like eating but I remained on edge. I still expected Lyall to turn up out of the blue and drag me away. I didn't believe my family would let me go. Lyall and Tony were the same as my father, ruthless men who thought of me as a commodity to make money. However, when Patricia asked me if I wanted to go to Malado with her again, I happily agreed.

We dressed carefully and this time I entered the place with anticipation instead of dread. Inside, we went to the table, the same one as before; we listened to the wonderful music and drank our coffee and it felt wonderfully calm. Patricia revealed she had spoken to the doctor.

'He says you need to be educated to live in the world Mary – that I should show you life – that you have a brain and need to use it - to be able to make your own decisions until you find your own identity.'

Decisions? Identity? I've always agreed and said, 'yes' to everyone – 'yes Mother' - 'yes Lyall' - 'yes Tony.' … I only knew to say 'yes' … I've always tried to please at any cost … Hey … but then, I had actually said 'no' to Tony. Maybe I can make decisions? My own identity? Don't know … can I?

Patricia and I surveyed the people, laughing and dancing to the music, people at ease, people drinking coffee. I sensed someone near me and looked up to see a trim, tall young man standing at our table. A handsome Bavarian gentleman, he looked at me and smiled.

'Hello - please excuse me introducing myself. My name is Eberhard Tinschert. I'm from Munich in Germany.' He clicked his heels and continued. 'May I ask you, young lady, would you care to dance?'

In astonishment, I shook my head, reddened, and eyes downcast, replied abruptly, 'I don't dance.'

Patricia smiled and explained. 'I'm sorry to interrupt but Mary is recovering from a sickness. I bought her here as she's never been to a dance. She doesn't dance.'

'Oh …' The dashing young man smiled back and said, 'You young ladies look so lovely – oh well … I'll leave you then.' He clicked his heels again and turned away, back to his table of friends.

'Why would he ask me?' I questioned Patricia in bewilderment.

'Because he wanted to.'

I shook my head. 'I can't do that.'

'One day you will,' she replied as we drank our coffee and continued to listen to the music.

After another week of the doctor's injections I was still not eating a meal and continued to need to have a door in sight so I could leave a room if I needed. I always marked out where the exit was – I still expected someone to jump out in front of me and drag me back … back to the Buchanan house … back to being a slave … but gradually I became a little more confident.

During the day, Betty suggested I go for a walk round the block and one sunny day I agreed. I had begun to feel less anxious and, I suppose, had slowly begun to grow into my personality. As I walked along, a car pulled up and the driver asked if I knew where Smith Street was. About to shake my head, I remembered I knew where it was – *Betty and Bob live in Smith Street.* I explained directions and he asked if I wanted a lift. I refused and before driving off, he smiled knowingly from the driver's seat and said 'Shame …I'm just going to visit Bob.'

My heart seemed to beat doubly fast - petrified with fright I found my way back to the Smith Street house and told Betty what had happened. She confirmed no-one was due to visit. When I told Patricia that night, she knew it was a warning.

'Time we moved on,' she declared.

In despair I asked where to, and she replied 'Newtown. It's a district close to the doctor and my work. We will have to leave the boys here but …' I shook my head protesting but she continued 'it's only until we get settled. I can't tell you anymore just yet but keep calm. I have plans.'

I continued with my doctor's visits, aware that Lyall's people might be watching out for me, and I lost some of my new-found exuberance. However, when Patricia told me we were going out again on Friday night, it gave me something to look forward to.

We arrived at the Malado Cafe, and I felt quite confident going in. Patricia laughingly said, 'you've walked in here faster than me this time Mary.'

We sat at our 'usual' table and calming music filled the room. Catching sight of us, the tall, trim young man from last week approached, and clicked his heels again. 'Hello, remember me? Eberhard Tinschert.'

Smiling, Patricia and I nodded. He regarded me with a searching expression, and said 'And how are you feeling tonight? Would you care to try to dance with me, Mary? Just try... if you don't like it, you can come back here.'

I sat speechless, staring up at him. 'Umm ...' I shook my head. He put out his hand and said 'I'm not going to hurt you ... just stand ... I'll guide you.'

I looked at Patricia and she nodded, so, quite terrified, I stood up and walked with him to the tiny dance floor. As the sweet music continued, he put his arm around me and guided me to the music tempo. 'Do you feel all right?' he asked. 'You shake a lot ... like a butterfly.'

Trembling and feeling quite uncomfortable, I swayed to the music next to him and replied, 'I've been very sick.'

The music stopped and he continued to hold my arm and we made our way back to Patricia.

'The music is very good here. May I see you here again Mary?'

Unnerved, I reacted quickly saying 'Um ... no, I'm a married woman with little children.'

By this time we were back standing at our table and Patricia looked up at us ... enquiringly.

'She sure shakes a lot,' the young man said to her.

Patricia answered, 'She's been brutalised and has been very ill.'

He turned to go but before he left, he said 'Well, she's very pretty and if she has little children, they must also be beautiful like their mother.' Eberhard smiled at us both, clicked his heels, and left.

Patricia whispered, 'You don't have to tell anyone you're married, Mary,' but I just sat dumbfounded, watching Eberhard retreat to his friends. *He seems a nice person - he seems kind. He only wanted to dance with me … but … I'm just too afraid.*

For some months, Patricia and I continued to go to the dance on a Friday evening and Eberhard became a regular at our table and I danced slowly with him and really enjoyed it. Patricia had briefly explained to him my predicament due to past history. I wanted her to stop but she told him I needed help and he became even more sympathetic, wanting to assist in any way he could. He introduced me to his European friends and, with his patience and encouragement, taught me many things. He was always kind and completely different to any man I had met and never tried to touch me. He was to become a true friend.

I continued to attend my appointments with Doctor Stulzman and receive intravenous injections, as he tried to correct the years of damage that malnutrition had done to my body. He asked about my food intake, but I explained I could still only eat small amounts. He was gentle but insistent. 'We will continue with the injections, but they can't go on forever - it's not natural. You will have to try to learn to eat – just like you taught your children to eat when you showed them love, Mary. This is love … love is caring and cherishing.'

Then he asked about my progress in getting out and about and I explained that Patricia and I had been going to a weekly dance venue. He encouraged me to continue and confirmed that it was good for my mind as well as my body.

'This is the start of your new life Mary, and if you take it slowly, stimulate your brain as well as your body, you will soon be like Patricia, able to live independently and work and look after yourself and your children. Learning to eat is just the start. So … how old are you now?'

'I found out my age in hospital years ago. A doctor told me I was thirteen – my parents had never mentioned it, so I've never thought about age.' I shrugged. 'Umm …I'm about twenty-nine, I think.'

'So, what does age mean to you, Mary?'

I thought hard before I answered. 'Nothing …nothing to me … only for my growing children.'

The doctor spoke slowly and quietly. 'Well your biological age is supposed to mean something, and you must continue to stimulate your brain outside in the world you know. At the moment you don't know who you really are but in time you will - and you will benefit and get to learn who you really are. You will become independent and not be afraid.'

I knew I was slowly regaining my confidence and my life. I now had friends who I thought of as my new family and they, unlike my old family, only wanted goods things for me. I wanted to be like Patricia. For the first time, I knew I would fight back if my biological family sent someone to grab me. And this is exactly what happened one day, a few weeks later, leaving the doctor's surgery.

Making my way back to my car, I felt a thumb and index finger dig into me - an iron grip on the back of my neck. A menacing male voice, close to my ear, said smoothly, 'Hello Mary. I see you've been to the doctor, but you look fit enough to me – fit enough to come home.'

That old fear took hold again. I didn't recognise the voice but when I managed to swivel my head round, neither did I recognise the man's hostile face.

'Why didn't you just come up and just say "Hello," I croaked?

'No Mary, this is a better way. I've come to remind you that you are a married woman and need to return to your husband.'

Petrified, I replied, 'Women do leave their husbands.'

'No Mary - you are part of a contract – you know what a contract is, don't you Mary?' I nodded with difficulty, and he continued. 'You've broken that contract, Mary. I've been selected to tell you to return to Lyall. He may be the world's most stupid man with his gambling problems, but your mother and father are not stupid. You are married until you or Lyall, one of you, dies or divorces. You and Lyall are both alive and you cannot divorce, 'cos you will lose your children. Your little boys are thriving, and you wouldn't want Bob and Betty to have a visit from one of your father's friends.'

'They've done nothing wrong,' I gasped, suddenly gripped by a wave of fear..

His voice was ominous. 'Oh yes they have. If you try to divorce, the family will tell the courts you're an unfit mother and take your boys. The contract stands Mary – return to Lyall and you will be able to see your little girl again.'

'If I were to come back, would I get my little girl back?' I asked cowering away from him.

The man bristled and replied through gritted teeth. 'I didn't say that, and I don't think you're in a position to bargain.' With that he smacked me in the face and walked off, bellowing as he walked, 'Now you stupid girl, go home to your husband.'

My head spinning, I tasted blood and realised it was coming from my nose and tried to stop the blood streaming down my face. I soaked a handkerchief with water from a nearby garden tap and mopped up the blood – ready to say I'd 'run into a tree' if anyone asked, but nobody approached me. No-one offered to help. Trying to focus, I stood shivering before returning to the car. I knew, no matter what everyone said, I wasn't free...*I'll never be free.*

Back home, I told Patricia what had happened. She told me she thought we should move on but leave the children with Betty and Bob as they were happy and safe. I didn't want to leave my children, but we couldn't move them with us, and I knew people were after me. *Staying will be dangerous* - she later told me there had been some strangers seen hanging around outside the house.

With the boys enrolled in school, Betty and Bob were happy to look after them and agreed to a new plan. Patricia and I quietly slid out of the Smith Street house at night and moved to a house in

Newtown, an old working-class area. Our new home in Clara Street didn't appear much from the outside – a small, rather run-down, two storey terraced house – but inside it was clean and comfortable, complete with basic furniture and bedding, enough for the two of us. It was owned by friends of Patricia who had come from overseas. They too had seen hard times so were sympathetic. I asked Patricia about the rent, and she shrugged and told me she had savings.

I felt embarrassed and answered, 'But Patricia, you can't continue to support me; I have to get a job.'

She brushed my worry away with, 'The rent here is small so we can stay for a while. It's near my work and you have to concentrate on getting well.'

I felt so grateful to her and told her so. Patricia smiled, a gentle smile, and explained 'Mary, actually you're helping me too. My son doesn't want to talk to me as his father has told him lies – convinced him that I'm not a good mother - and I used to feel so depressed. I had nothing to live for. Then I met you again and you gave me a purpose – to free you. So you are actually helping me get through my sadness.'

✳ ✳ ✳

I continued going to the doctor, still ate only small amounts of food and we were still spending Friday evenings at the Malado, By this time Eberhard had become a frequent visitor to our table, always asking how I was and offering to buy our coffees. He quickly become a friend and Patricia and I agreed that we both liked him. One evening he explained his wanting to support me.

'I would be happy to take you out for a drive – for coffee, for a ride to nice scenic places. Patricia is invited too, of course.'

Bemused, I asked why, and he said, 'Well, I like to help people and … I've fallen for you.'

Patricia smiled and agreed to his offer, and I nodded too. He seemed a gentle soul and we both enjoyed his company. One day he took us to show us where he lived in Mosman. It was a large, house on Sydney's wealthy north shore, owned by a German lady. She rented rooms to a number of young men from Germany and Yugoslavia and Eberhard introduced us to them. They all clicked their heels (a German sign of respect) on introduction, and we felt very special. Then we met an elegant older lady, the house owner - Frau Metchler, who welcomed us.

'Yes, I know all about you two. You are Patricia and you are Mary. Eberhard has told me your history. You have a pretty face and lovely hair Mary – you look like a gypsy – but you're far too thin. I'll make us some coffee but' she turned to Eberhard, saying 'make sure she eats something.'

Well, he did - cutting tiny pieces of salami – a bit for him and a bit for me. He ate a morsel, then I ate, and I liked it - and I didn't feel sick. Next came tiny pieces of cheese – a bit for him and a bit for me. I ate the cheese and liked it too – and again I didn't feel sick. Patricia looked on, happy to see me eating and Frau Metchler too, who said, 'I'm going to call you Gypsy – the name suits you.'

Eberhard took Patricia and I for a few rides and soon he began to call in regularly to our Clare Street house. One evening he brought some chocolate and asked why we were living in the Clare Street house – although it was convenient it wasn't particularly homely. Patricia explained my need for safety and Eberhard looked visibly upset. Over the weeks, he became a regular visitor, each time bringing things for me to eat, gently encouraging me with small bites of chocolate, or cheese, or salami. Whilst I found I liked the tastes I could still only eat a mouthful without feeling ill.

One day Eberhard took me for a ride to Sydney's north shore and I noticed he had placed small amounts of cheese on the dashboard for me to eat. I really liked this cheese and began to indulge but I was soon doubled over, with a great stomach-ache.

The pains worsened and fearing I had a serious problem, Eberhard found a medical centre and took me in to see a doctor. After questioning me, the doctor said she thought the likely cause of my pains was from eating all that cheese. It had brought on a bad case of indigestion.

From that lesson, I learned not to over-indulge and Eberhard learned not to over-feed me. When I told Patricia she laughed and said, 'You're really are learning to eat if you are suffering indigestion!'

After a short time, Eberhard came up with a plan for both me and Patricia. A friend owned a boarding house in nearby Marrickville. The housekeeper was returning to Poland, and he needed someone to keep the place clean and tidy. Eberhard said there were six men and two women who lived there. They all worked and led sober lives – no drinking or fighting. Would I be interested in the housekeeper's job which came with two large rooms and a small wage?

Patricia and I discussed it and it was decided that it would be good for us both. She would move with me into one of the housekeeper's large rooms, and I would be doing housework – the same as I had always done but this time, I would be receiving a wage. I still received intravenous nutrition from the doctor, but I had enough energy to do housework. I agreed and went for the interview.

The job was mine and with Eberhard's help, Patricia and I moved into the spacious housekeeper's rooms in the boarding house, and I parked my car in the garage. My job consisted of ensuring all the boarders were woken and left for work and to look after the property, which consisted mainly of cleaning the communal areas. I had usually finished by eleven in the morning and then went to see Doctor Stulzman, I told him about my new living arrangements and my job, and he was delighted. He also told me I should be seeking a job outside my confining horizons – something to awaken my hidden abilities.

'Something to stimulate your mind – something that will slowly bring you into the real world and make you a free woman … but go slow, Mary. You are not physically strong yet. I know you haven't told me all the things that happened in your past, but I can see you have painful memories locked inside you. You need to find out who you really are, Mary.'

His advice echoed in my head. *Who am I? I really don't know who I am.* I went back to the boarding house and thought about what the good doctor had said.

Now Eberhard came to visit most evenings after work, and he asked me if he could teach me to dance. I felt hesitant – *what benefit will it be to me?* He explained I should learn to do many things to make myself more confident and one of them was to dance to music and take away some of my fears. I knew I would be afraid forever. He said 'Mary, in my country your name would be pronounced 'Maria' – would you mind if I called you that?

I thought about it … *'Maria'* … the name sounded pretty, almost melodic, and I agreed. As time went by, Eberhard became more and more aware of my background from speaking to Patricia. "What sort of people treat you like a slave and feed you scraps? I've never heard of such a thing. Now I understand more why you have to learn to eat.'

As time went by, Eberhard turned into a dear friend and he became fonder of me, often bringing me chocolates. When I thanked him one day, he said 'Love is caring and sharing Maria. If you were free, I'd ask you to marry me.'

Hmm, I thought, well I'm not and I wouldn't. I don't want to be married ever again. I've had enough of that. I just want to be me.

Eberhard must have read my thoughts as, in a quiet voice he continued. 'You don't love me yet Maria but, in time, you will – you will think outside the memories of slavery and cruelty you have endured.'

The weeks passed and one weekend, Eberhard took Patricia and I to meet his friends. He explained they were a European group who were meeting at the home of Tessa. We arrived and were introduced by Eberhard as Patricia and Maria. I quite liked being called Maria. It seemed more interesting than plain 'Mary.' The sound of beautiful music floated through the house, and one of the friends, Vera Goldman, began to dance.

Well, I was mesmerised as she danced and swayed to the Latin music. Vera continued to dance around the room and came towards me, pulling me near with the scarf around my neck. A little apprehensive, I tried to mimic her steps and followed Vera's movements - gradually she danced away and left me swaying, following the music. I had often seen my mother dance around the house, 'en pointe' in her ballet shoes, but this was the first time I myself had done anything like a dance. When the music stopped, so did I and Tessa clapped and told me how good I was. One of the friends, Frau Metchler, the lady who had called me a gypsy –'Maria the gypsy'– asked if I could sing, and I shook my head vehemently. I told them I didn't.

'I would have thought you'd be a good singer going by your speaking voice,' Tessa said.

I just shook my head again. Mrs Buchanan used to get me out of bed, in the wee small hours, to sing to her drunken boarder and his friends. I couldn't be persuaded to sing under any circumstances – it would bring back all those terrible times. The expression of terror on my face must have told them not to pursue the suggestion. They were all very gentle with me that day and I was truly grateful and happy to be in the company of this European group..

At another gathering held at a friend of Eberhard's, a beautiful house with a grand piano, Vera sat and played the most hauntingly delightful music and I sensed it move me – I felt at peace. Later we sat down at the table for lunch. Each person had a cutlet and some salad, and without thinking, I started to eat what was put in front of me. I ate the cutlet and salad as if I had done it all my life. I didn't look at the food, just ate, as I listened to the conversations around me. It seemed so natural as if I'd always eaten this way. It dawned on me that I didn't feel sick whilst Eberhard and Patricia stared at me quite bewildered. The food tasted wonderful ... *perhaps the music has healed me.*

After the meal, we were gathered together talking and I wandered over to a large glass-fronted antique wooden cabinet containing an exquisite violin. *Isn't that the most beautiful thing,* I thought as I stood, gazing at it in wonder.

Tessa joined me at the cabinet saying, 'I don't play violin anymore – since I had a health episode, my hands don't work well.' Carefully opening the glass door she took out the violin and offered the musical instrument to me. 'Want to try?' she asked.

'Oh ... I can't ...I don't play,' I replied bewildered, but she said, 'just try.' She showed me how to hold the violin and murmured encouragement. 'See what sound you can make.'

I held this wonderful violin in my hands and so wanted to make music but didn't know what to do. She repeated 'just try.'

I don't know how I did it, and it wasn't beautiful sounds that emerged, but I played – the bow kept doing the correct things. Tessa, Eberhard, and Patricia were astounded and just stared at me.

Tessa asked, 'Who taught you the violin?'

I shrugged, 'no one – my mother played guitar and could dance 'en pointe' but I never, ever ...'

'What did you feel – playing the violin?' she asked.

I thought about it. *What had I felt?* 'It was sweet ...and really delightful ... but I've never touched a violin ... or even played anything before.'

Tessa looked astounded. 'Well Maria, you have a gift - something special inside you waiting to get out. You and my violin belong together. I must endeavour to follow through – Maria you really have a special talent. It took me years to get those same delightful notes out of the violin.'

Eberhard bounded over to my side and pulled me into his arms, holding me tight. 'I told you – you really are special' he whispered. 'Something incredible happened here. A door in your life has started to open.'

Later Eberhard said 'You are still very ill and need more treatment, but you must think of us all as your relatives. Mary has gone. You are now Maria, and we all love you - we are your new family.'

This had never happened before – it felt strange, and I reached out and stroked his hand. I'd never had anyone say they loved me. I felt a hurt and touched my chest with my hands. I told him about my pain and Eberhard said it was my heart – my feelings had been awakened.

'Soon you will be able to live without medication, Maria.'

I smiled but I wasn't so sure about that. I had often wondered if I would ever be able to live a normal life, but I knew something incredible had happened to me. I couldn't explain it, but it was a momentous thing.

Many years later, together with a violin master, I was shown techniques which allowed me to play but this actual day remains a day of never-forgotten joy – the day the violin and I came together.

* * *

CHAPTER 6

THINKING FOR MYSELF

I still didn't feel free of my family, but I had started to think for myself and devise a plan for the day. I had earned sufficient money to go to visit Betty and Bob and pay something towards my children's up-keep. At the same time, and even more importantly, I would see my three darling little boys. I decided to take the car out of the garage and park it in front of the house. *That way, if anyone is watching me, they'll think I'm at home.* Even though I couldn't see anyone loitering, I knew my father's contacts were sneaky and would blend into the surroundings – *after all, they're professionals – professional criminals and stand-over men..*

I wrote Patricia a note to say I was leaving the car and walking to visit the boys. I scrutinised the pavements outside – there were few people around - so I set out on foot, continually checking over my shoulder for anyone following me. I managed to find my way to Betty and Bob's house and had a delightful, joyful reunion with my boys who seemed to be thriving in their calm, happy environment.

Too soon it was almost dusk, and I headed for home – enjoying the walk and the freedom. Still terribly thin and weak, I felt I had become stronger, but I was tiring as I neared home; I knew I'd had enough.

From the shadows of a laneway, a man stepped out and took my arm in a firm hold. 'You're coming with me,' he said in a harsh, thick Italian accent. 'You're coming back with me.'

'No!' I cried out, alarmed … trying to pull away.

'Don't say 'no.' You have done wrong by them. Don't cause attention now. You are coming,' he declared firmly, clasping my arm even tighter and pulling me close.

At that moment a young couple stepped out of their house and, taking advantage of their presence, I pulled my arm away from the man, and turned, shouting 'See you another time, bye,' as I sprinted away and dodged down a side street into the main road. Head down, I ran as fast as my legs would carry me, glancing up as I slowed. To my dismay, I found the man in front of me, menacing me with something in his hand - a flick knife. Terrified, I looked around and saw a sign 'Police Station' and rushed forward, up the steps and through the doors. *I'm safe*, I thought with relief. *This is Ashfield Police Station,* as I burst through the doors into the foyer. At the desk, a young constable scanned my flushed, frightened face and asked me what was wrong.

Flustered, my heart beating madly, I gasped out 'that man … outside …at the gate … is going to knife me.'

He asked me if I knew him.

'He's a friend of my husband,' I gasped.

He sat me on a nearby chair and the phone rang. As he went to answer it, a sergeant came into the foyer, saw me, and asked him, pointing in my direction, 'What's she doing here – what's the story?'

Phone call completed, the constable explained that a man had chased me with a knife. The sergeant glared around outside and couldn't see anyone hanging about. He turned to me and growled 'Don't come in here with your petty spats. Get out before I charge you with loitering.'

I told him the man would kill me. The policeman answered in a steely voice - 'come back when he does.'

Reluctantly I left the station, walking down the steps and checking around. I couldn't see the Italian, so again I turned and dashed towards home. I must have appeared terrified as, a few doors away, a blonde woman about to go inside her house, looked at me enquiringly as I ran towards her on the street. She asked me what was wrong.

'There's a man chasing me,' I panted, and she grabbed my arm and pulled me inside the building, hurriedly shutting the door. Exhausted and scared, I nearly collapsed, and she helped me to a chair to get my breath back.

She sat me down and asked, 'What's going on?'

As my breathing became calmer, I explained what had happened – being chased by a large Italian man and at the police station. She listened intently then grew angry.

'Ugg … men! What …? Told you to come back when you're stabbed … I'm disgusted with the police's attitude. What do I pay my rates for? Look, I'll make a cup of tea. You're safe now - I have a car and can drive you home afterwards. Would you like that?'

I thanked her for being so understanding and gradually I stopped shaking. As I drank my tea, I shared a fragment of my history, adding, 'I've been ill.'

She told me she too had been in hospital and the cause had been an Italian man, a sweetheart who had used and then dropped her. She hadn't wanted to live and had taken an overdose but had been revived in hospital. In the process, her larynx had been cut and she's ended up with a gravelly voice - 'Italian's can be really vicious.'

When I calmed down, she drove me home and came inside with me to ensure I felt well enough to cope. Patricia had already returned from work and my new friend revealed to her what happened to me and how we'd met. After she left, Patricia seemed upset with me.

'Why didn't you tell me they were still around? I didn't know they'd followed you here. You didn't say anything.'

I motioned I was sorry. 'I didn't want you to worry, Patricia. I've been expecting something to happen. These people won't change.'

That evening, Eberhard was furious when he heard what had happened and how the police had reacted.

I too was beside myself with frustrated anger. 'You don't understand. I can't stay here. It will happen again. These people are ruthless … violent … my father has power, and I don't want to put you two in danger.'

Eberhard shook his head in disbelief. 'You can't go back. You don't want to be a slave. You're free.'

But I'm not … they just don't understand - I'll never be free.

∗ ∗ ∗

For a month or two I kept a low profile, just leaving the house in my car to see the doctor for my injections. I cleaned the communal areas and the rest of the house, but I felt different to before. I realised I now knew what to do and could function on my own – I didn't need instructions – but I was always fearful. The anxiety laid me low, kept me awake at night, gave me nightmares, intruded into my thoughts. I hardly drove the car and there were days when I wasn't at all well … too ill to do much and Eberhard visited after his work; he would sit beside me and sing German lullabies to soothe me. He was so gentle and kind, but I knew it wasn't that simple. I felt it was all so hopeless. *Here I am, a grown woman, and baby songs calm me,* I thought. I was in despair. I knew my boys were happy but I missed and worried about Michele – there was an empty space when I thought about her.

One evening I said to Patricia and Eberhard, 'Maybe I should try to find some more work to fill in my afternoons. That might help me to find who I really am … but what will I do?'

They saw I was starting to think things through and agreed. 'You could work in a shop' was Patricia's answer, so that evening, we examined the newspaper 'wanted' adverts and came across a part-time vacancy – a salesperson wanted for a nearby shop called Silhouette, selling wigs to women who had lost their hair due to illness. It was a big step for me, but I wanted to try for it. Next day I applied – and wonders of wonder, I was offered the position.

I enjoyed the speaking to the customers and making them feel better about themselves. I showed them what to do, helping them try on various wigs - different styles and colours. I soon settled in to cleaning the boarding house in the morning, and the afternoon sales job, and after a couple of months, I began to feel a little more confident - things were going well. This was spoilt one afternoon after work as I approached my car - a woman took my arm, on one side, and a man took the other arm. They held me strong and fast.

'Let's go and have coffee' one said as they lifted me off my feet, dragging me towards a nearby van. They opened the doors and hastily shoved me inside, grazing my leg on the van floor.

As I yelped in pain the man's threatening voice said 'Shut up. You've caused enough trouble. They're all waiting for you - Lyall, Tony, your father and your big brothers.'

In terror I cried out 'I don't want to go back. I'll die – something dreadful will happen.'

The man's coarse voice was unconcerned. 'There's money involved – you must have known. We're just doing a job – we're being paid to take you home.'

'But ...' I stopped pleading as the van door slammed shut. It was dark and uncomfortable inside as I heard them walk around the front, open the doors, and climb into the driver and passenger seats. In horror, I knew I had to do something. In the blackness I stared at the closed van door. *I have to get out.* In terror, I pushed hard against the door handle, and, to my amazement, the door swung open. As the van slowly reversed, I quickly flung myself out, landing on my feet with a thud ... and ran. In terror, I sprinted into the nearest opening - a door of a building which led into the Bankstown shopping centre – and raced into the ladies' toilet block. It was empty and I locked myself into a toilet stall, sitting on the toilet lid until my heart stopped pounding. I used some toilet paper to stop the blood trickling down my leg and stayed in there for a long time.

The only safe way is to be with people, I thought, so, when I heard a group, talking and passing outside, I rushed out of the toilets into the centre of the crowd. Walking in the middle of the throng, I looked around and couldn't see anyone watching for me. Blood was bleeding down into my shoe, but no-one seemed to notice. I kept walking, slowly, mixing in with the crowd as we went along the street towards home. My heart beating madly, I managed to get back to the boarding house, and in my room, I cleaned up the blood again and, exhausted, I sat to think.

They won't leave me alone. No-one must know but I've got to go. I have to get away – no packing, just up and go.

About to walk out the front door, I met a smiling Eberhard, dressed in his usual attire - a smart jacket and trousers, neat shirt with a cravat - striding up the front path towards me.

'Hello… where're you going?' he asked surprised … 'and what's happened to your leg, Maria?' I glanced down and saw the cut on my leg was bleeding again. I shrugged and, looking concerned he continued, 'Let's go back inside and you can tell me.'

He towered over me, not moving aside, so defeated, I turned back into the house and Eberhard followed behind – there was to be no escape.

'Let's make a cup of tea and you can tell me what happened,' he said in a questioning voice.

At the table, I sat downcast. Hot tea in hand, he asked 'Now what happened? Did you fall down somewhere?'

I sipped my tea and, not meeting his eyes, said 'Yes.'

In disbelief he asked 'Oh really? Now I want you to tell me the real truth.'

So, upset, I opened up, and the story came pouring out. I told him how I had nearly been kidnapped.

Eberhard was furious. 'This is a police matter, Maria.'

'It will only stir things up' I replied in despair. 'The police haven't helped me before.'

Eberhard agreed but he was really concerned. 'Well, I think it is time you stopped working here. I will have to find somewhere else for you.'

'It's not your concern. You don't want to get involved,' I replied, feeling embarrassed.

'Well, as far as I'm concerned, I am involved. I really care about you.'

'But … I'm a married woman,' I said weakly.

Eberhard gestured he didn't agree. 'Only because you're not yet divorced. I'll be here for you Maria.'

Just then Patricia came home, and he told her what had happened. My leg continued to bleed as they talked.

'We must get that cut attended to … stop any infection.'

So I was whisked off to Doctor Stulzman's surgery where he checked and dressed the wound. Giving me a tetanus shot, he listened as Eberhard and Patricia explained how I had come to be injured.

'This is becoming a criminal matter,' he said seriously. Fearfully I replied 'Yes, that's what Eberhard said, but please don't.'

I was adamant I didn't want the police involved. The last thing I wanted was all my secrets laid bare for everyone to know. Things began to move quite fast after that.

* * *

Eberhard and Maria

Eberhard and Maria's wedding day

Vera

New South Wales Dept. of Corrective Services

Jenny Craig consultant

Me playing the violin

The Civic Centre, Bankstown, Sydney

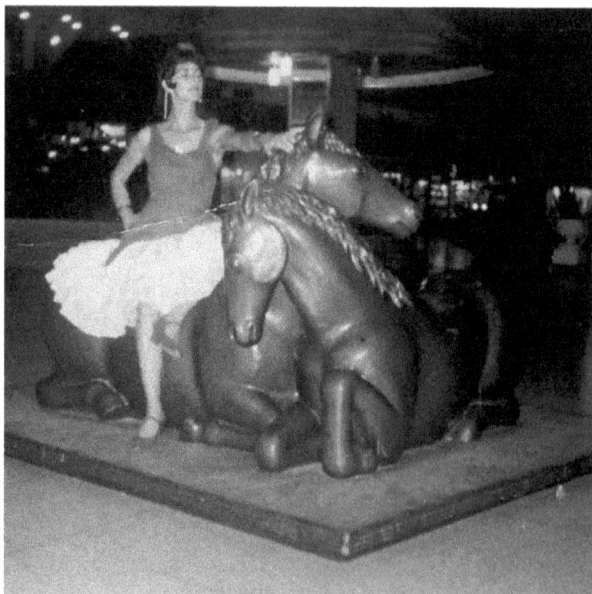

Opening Roselands Shopping Centre, Sydney

Grand Old Opre, Penrith, Sydney

At Dreamworld

Me and Eberhard

TWEED HEADS FIRE STATION
THE PEOPLE SAY
THANK YOU MARIA
WITH THE ROSE
IN HER HAIR

Air Sea Rescue & State Emergency Services

The Salvation Army - Red Shield Appeal.

THE
SALVATION
ARMY

Certificate
of
Recognition

This certificate is presented to

MARIA TINSCHERT

in recognition of service through the
Community Care Ministries of The Salvation Army.

David Godkin (Lt-Colonel)
Divisional Commander, Queensland

14 September 2020

At the launch of Daughter of the Razor
Book 1, Gold Coast 2016

Me and Ralph James

CHAPTER 7

GYPSY

Well readers, my greatest lesson of all was taking place. What is love? I had no answers as I had never experience love before – not from my mother, my family members or anyone – and suddenly here I was receiving love from people who loved me, recent acquaintances, and friends … and they didn't expect any kind of payment.

One day Eberhard showed me how much he cared – he suggested it was time we seriously thought about my future. He knew I had a long way to go but thought, maybe, I could be reunited with my children and live together with them in a house on my own. He hesitantly asked me for my own thoughts on this next step.

'Would you like to live in a nearby suburb with your children, Maria? – no strings attached, of course. Neither I nor Patricia would live with you. It would have to be near work, but would you like to set up on your own?'

I nodded, excited at the thought. *Oh yes - on my own, with my children!*

Patricia was nearby, listening. She was hesitant but pleased to see I was enthusiastic, exclaiming, 'Well, this is amazing. You must be feeling so much better. See how far you've come Mary.'

I smiled but in actual fact, I was not anywhere near ready to step out on my own. I pretended I felt free for sweet Patricia and

Eberhard's sake but, deep in the recess of my mind, I knew I would never be free of my family, never be safe, and silently wondered if it truly was too soon to step out alone.

Eberhard once again showed his caring friendship by finding me a house near Burwood but seemed quite worried for me. He knew I would encounter a world I had no experience with and this time I would be on my own. I quickly settled in but was frightened at taking responsibility for the children just yet. I needed some time to come to terms with this latest step, sometime for myself, before uprooting the boys and trying to get my little girl back into the family fold.

My new friend Tessa knew I enjoyed dancing and suggested I try to express my creative side and find who I was before settling down. She told me she thought I should apply to dance in a Sydney production she'd read about. Peter Weir, an Australian Director, was in the process of seeking dancers for Carmen, the opera. She suggested I go and apply.

'I don't expect you to do it alone. Vera has offered to take you to the audition.'

'But I'm not a dancer – not a real dancer,' I countered in dismay.

'You can dance Maria - you are special - all your friends agree. Simply walk in … you are perfect for the role. Just walk in and tell them you're the gypsy they're looking for.'

Vera and I set off for the city. Nervous and in a daze, I entered the ABC building and asked for the Peter Weir auditions. I was directed to a huge hall where dozens of girls were lined up. I walked past them as I saw the great man himself, Peter Weir, was in his glass-walled office with four or five people.

I didn't hesitate and walked in and stood directly in front of Peter. Everyone in the office stopped talking and stared at me. Surprised, he peered up at me and asked, 'Yes? What can I do for you?'

I looked him in the eye and replied, 'You're looking for a gypsy for the opera Carmen. I'm your gypsy.'

The room seemed very quiet. Around me, people waited with

bated breath to see what was about to unfold. Slowly, Peter stood up and told me to turn around and I did.

He asked, 'Do you sing?'

I shook my head and answered 'I can, but I don't want to. I can dance though.'

Puzzled, he stared at me. 'So you want to be in the opera?'

'Yes please.'

Motioning to the people watching outside, he answered with a sigh, 'You see all these ladies? They all want a part too.'

Head held high, I replied haughtily 'But I'm who I am – a gypsy and you want a gypsy who can dance.'

He grinned and picked up a couple of blue sheets of paper, saying, 'Do you know the role of Manuelita.'

I shrugged. I didn't.

'She's Carmen's rival. You can be Manuelita … no singing - no words – just dance and act. Here's a contract.'

Clutching the contract, I left the room in a daze and made my way back out of the building. Outside, Vera waited, and I walked towards her holding out the sheets of blue paper.

'Did you see Peter Weir? Did you get it, the dance role,' Vera asked in astonishment …'the role of a factory worker?'

I shook my head – 'no, but I got the role of Manuelita. Look, here's my contract.'

'Manuelita? But … but she's Carmen's rival…how did you…?'

Vera was ecstatic and we drove home discussing how lucky I had been. She couldn't wait to tell Eberhard and Patricia.

I enjoyed my part in the show which took quite a few days to film in northern Sydney. In one scene, I was directed to stand, hands on hips, and viciously spit at Carmen and in another I spent some time in the make-up chair whilst they crafted a realistic scar on my face from a supposed fight with Carmen, the star (played by Janine Arnou). Little did they realise that underneath my make-up was the memory of real scars on my mother's victims. When the journalist and photographer from Woman's Weekly came to the suburb of Woolloomooloo to take the casts' photographs and write the advertorial, I stayed as quiet as I could. The last thing I needed was a spread showing my name and face. I never watched the show on television.

Eberhard and Patricia worried things were happening too fast for me to cope; they sensed I was like an out-of-control train on the track. Actually, despite my nervousness, I didn't show it and tried to feel calm and confident so I could face the world. All I wanted to do was work to make money ... money for my future and the children. I had a goal – I wanted to see my children safe and live without violence and fear..

Patricia wasn't surprised at my success. 'You are incredibly special Mary. It's happening because you're using your brain which had been underused for so long.'

By this time I was meeting all sorts of people, international people, through Vera as she invited people from different countries for drinks. At one get-together, she had danced to the beat of a lone drummer, and I watched mesmerised. Later we discussed dancing and she told me 'that's how you dance. I think you should be called Attara – not change your real name but use it as a stage name. You are a very good Moorish and Spanish dancer.'

'Oh ... Attara ... why?'

'Attara – it sounds like a tiara, a crown. When you dance it's not as Maria but as Attara, someone special. You're a queen from television.'

That week, a group of us were to attend a night at Spanish club to watch well-known dancers, Michael Gilmore, and his partner Veronica. At the last moment, they cancelled due to illness and the manager came to our table and told Vera he had no dancers; she was asked whether she would dance. She declined but introduced 'a very special dancer'– Maria Duano was the name she called me as a Spanish dancer - suggesting I take their place.

I was hesitant but Vera insisted I was ready to perform. I just lost myself as I danced to the music of a Flamenco guitarist. After seeing me perform my Flamenco dance, the manager offered me a job at the club. I'd glance around and could see people applauding wildly and I had to ask myself if I was dreaming. I seemed to be living someone else's life … I gradually began to feel content and more secure. *A dancer I must be.*

After a while, Eberhard asked me again 'Do you want to have the children live with you?'

I ached to have them with me, but I didn't think it safe yet. I knew the family would be watching – waiting, but Eberhard insisted my awful family had probably become used to my being lost to them. Patricia too insisted they would not be looking for me.

'Besides, they know what they did was illegal, and they can't force you to return. They'd be arrested if they tried to do anything to you or the children.'

I was never convinced and knew the future wouldn't be that simple and I was proved correct when one day there was a knock at the front door. Lulled into a feeling of security, I opened the door to find Mrs Buchanan, my mother inlaw, and her daughter Joyce standing there. My heart seemed to stop beating. It felt like I'd been hit by a truck.

'Oh hello Mary. Fantastic … we found you home. We need to talk to you.'

Alarmed, I had trouble finding my voice. 'How did you find me?' I croaked out.

'Oh … there are ways.'

'What's wrong?' I gasped, thinking '*accident*.' 'Is it Michele?'

Mrs Buchanan gave a creepy smile. 'No … no …Nothing like that… we were looking for you. Are we coming in or do we just stand here on the doorstep?'

Well readers, I'm sure you're thinking why is she allowing this to happen? Everyone – the doctor, Eberhard, Patricia – had continually told me I'm free of the Buchanans but my mind seemed to be out of my control. I don't know why but I reverted back – still under the influence of these people. I dutifully stepped aside and allowed them in.

Indoors, my in-laws settled themselves down as though they were treasured friends. I silently stared at them … waiting.

Mrs Buchanan was the first to speak. 'Well, it's like this Mary, Joyce and I want to move in with you.'

Am I dreaming? move… here … why? Unable to think straight, I gasped out 'What?'

'We want to move in with you – here,' she repeated.

'… oh but you can't,' I spluttered. Their two pasty faces stared back at me as I continued 'My friend pays for this house.'

'Aah … a friend …really?' came the reply. 'A he or she?'

'No… it's not …. he's not … I live here on my own.'

'So … this is a kind of payment, is it?' Mrs Buchanan hissed. 'And where are the children?'

I shook my head. 'No … nothing like that. I have … um, I work … and the children aren't here. They're safe.'

It felt like I was once again back in the Buchanan house … they're telling me what to do … calling me names … bullying … *but I'm not owned … I'm free … everyone told me they can't …*

'How did you find me,' I asked?

Mrs Buchanan, a knowing smile on her face, spoke again. 'Oh we know all about you and your friends and who pays the rent here … now Mary, I've always had a soft spot for you ..'

A soft spot, I thought. *You were spiteful and cruel.* My nerves on edge, I wondered what was coming next as I sensed myself slowly slipping back … back under her control.

'We need a place to live for a few months …'

I felt myself quiver as she continued.

'and we want to move in here …'

'Move in … in here?' I heard myself ask in a fearful voice. 'But you can't. My friend pays the rent and …'

Mrs Buchanan's firm voice overrode me '… we still have Michele, remember … she'll come here with us … and Mary, I'm sure you can sort it out with your friend. We need to live somewhere.'

I stood stock still, unnerved, trying to take in what she'd said as she continued. 'We'll come back tomorrow. Don't shake your head. I think you'll let us – me, Joyce, and the little girls. After all, it was always Lyall that was the problem … and remember, we have Michele. In case any of your friends tell you otherwise, I know I wasn't awarded her through the courts but she's living under my roof.'

In a panic I protested. 'But … I don't pay the rent. It's paid by my friend. What do I tell him?'

'Just say you wanted us to live here. I know you will tell everyone we forced ourselves on you, but Michele is under my care, and we need to live somewhere - we'll be back tomorrow.' With that, she turned, and Joyce followed her, walking to the front door and out of the house.

I couldn't think straight. *How …why?*

I dreaded telling Eberhard but next day, when he came to visit, I had to tell him what had happened. 'Mrs Buchanan and Joyce are moving in and bringing Michele to live here.'

Eberhard just stood still and stared at me as he said, 'Did I hear you right.' His English was not perfect, and he seemed to be wondering if he had mis-heard me.

My voice quivered as I continued, 'Please don't get angry with me. They have Michele … I want her back … and … and they know everything … they know you rent the house for me … everything.'

Eberhard seemed thoughtful for a while then said quietly, 'I won't stand in your way Maria, I want to interfere, but I won't - but you must let Patricia know. Come - I will take you now.'

In silence, we drove to Patricia's home, and, like Eberhard, she looked really shocked when I told her Mrs Buchanan and Joyce were moving in and bringing my little girl to live with me.

Her shoulders drooped as she said, 'I won't stop you Mary, but I have to warn you this could be bad for you. You have to keep remembering they don't own you and the house is yours – and I will be watching.'

I nodded, relieved that it was no longer a secret.

'By the way, did you get the job' she asked?

I explained that I hadn't heard back but thought the job, as an assistant nurse at an old people's nursing home, was mine.

Eberhard didn't know what he could do to help me – after all, he loved me and wanted me to be happy and if having my daughter in the house made me happy, he accepted it. I did not understand 'love' and still have problems understanding the meaning of love.

* * *

Mrs Buchanan, Joyce, and Michele moved in that weekend. Mrs Buchanan surveyed the bedrooms and took the main room, informing me I could sleep in the little back bedroom. I didn't bother to argue, concentrating on greeting Michele, but she seemed to have changed. No longer was she happy, cuddly, and loving. She didn't ask where her brothers were or even try to talk to me. She was aloof and off-hand and I felt terribly sad but had no time to stop and think, I had begun the job at a nursing home.

Within a few days I was called to the matron's office who informed me the chef had taken ill and asked me whether I could cook. Next morning there I was with forty-eight eggs, making breakfast with toast. As Maria, I learned to cope but underneath it all I was still Mary – taking orders and watching how these elderly people were so cruelly treated. I saw the bad behaviour of the nursing staff to their elderly patients, moving them around, exposing their bodies to everyone's eyes, treating them without dignity or compassion. It made my skin crawl and in a short time I had to resign. But I wanted to work in this field, caring for people. I tried working at various homes in the Sydney area and found many were unfit and needed reporting to the authorities.

At one place I found the owner's husband was sexually assaulting the elderly women at night. I exposed one by phoning a radio station for help to report them. I saw the horror of the cruelty to these older citizens and the matrons didn't seem to care. I saw a nursing sister declare a person dead when she was still breathing and witnessed the cold showers the old people were forced into taking, their dignity ignored. Nobody seemed to care or wanted to know, and I couldn't continue to watch these things happen. I continued to report the atrocities and change jobs.

In the meantime, the Buchanans took over the house. I still did the housework and cooking as well as work outside the home. I was informed that Lyall was still happily working as a Taxi driver and taking his unpaid fares 'in kind.' It saddened me to see that Michele had become quite a spiteful little girl like the Buchanan family. Upset that they had such an impact on my daughter, I began to feel I had lost control again and was back under their influence. I needed advice and went to talk to Tess; I told her the entire story. Her answer went to the heart of the matter.

'This is all wrong Maria - these awful people staying in your house is wrong. This must be so hurtful to both Eberhard and Patricia. They worked so hard to get you away from that family.'

I knew this to be true and thought about taking up Eberhard's suggestion to work at his engineering factory. Eberhard knew working in residential care was taking a toll on me and that I could not sustain it. Eventually I said that it was too much seeing this cruelty to the elderly - I had to find another industry and he again invited me to work in his factory. I wanted to earn money for my children and agreed.

He decided he would move in with friends nearby, and drive with me to and from work in Drummoyne for a few weeks, to get me used to the journey. Gradually I knew the way and began to drive myself in my car. This company made specialist machinery for a government contract, and I was taught to work a lathe.

Eberhard reminded me that August was my birth month - my friends were about to make a big fuss for my birthday ... nobody had ever celebrated my birthday before. I was learning about life. It was all new to me but then, so was everything.

Around this time I had previously been employed at a nursing home. Now, I have known some wonderful people, but these were not that type. They must have had a connection to Tony, and he found my whereabouts. Tony wanted 'justice' and used his Mafia-like connections.

After work, on my way to my car to drive home, I was once again accosted by a man in the street. In a grip of steel from behind, I was slammed into a fence. In case anyone was watching him placing his hands around my throat, he kept up the pretence that he was my boyfriend, and we were making up after a spat. He dragged me into his car where he warned me to keep quiet, and told me he was going to talk some sense into me... I had to return to Lyall as his wife or there would be 'big consequences' – something awful would happen.

The threats were always against me and even worse, the unnamed consequences that would befall my children and, as these people were working for my father, who knew how depraved their actions could be. *I'm going to die – my children are safe but I'm going to die*, I thought.

In terror, my mind reverted to the brainwashing control and depression of my previous life – *I will never be free. My father sold me to the Buchanans. Lyall can get into as much debt as he wants if he can use me to repay his debts with sexual favours. He'll never let me go – I'm his money spinner. I'm never gonna' get them out of my life. They will always control me ... as they are now.*

In today's world, I would say 'Wake up to yourself and listen to your friends' good advice,' but, despite everything that had happened, despite having begun to build my self-confidence, the Buchanans mind-control lingered. *I'll never be free* was my thought, over and over in my mind.

Somehow, I managed to escape from his car and made my way home. When Eberhard came to visit, the house was quiet but straight away, he could see I was upset, even though I never shed a tear. Usually, I did not seem to feel things in the same way as others and kept my emotions from showing, but this time I must have looked upset. I explained what had happened and he was shocked.

'Oh mein liebchin, you're in real danger. What shall we do? We have to tell Patricia. We'll go now – come, we'll take my car.'

Straight back into the Buchanans' slave mode, I replied, 'Oh … I can't. I'm preparing a meal for Mrs Buchanan, I can't go,'

Eberhard disagreed. 'Damn Mrs Buchanan! Come with me – we are going to Patricia's – I'll drive… we have to discuss what's going on.'

At Patricia's, my heartbeat increased as Eberhard explained what had happened. She looked appalled. 'You could have been shot. We can't let you stay in that house with the Buchanans' Patricia gasped out.

Eberhard agreed. 'We will have to hide you somewhere – where they're not able to find you. Hmm … I know just the place. I have friends – the Littlejohns. They live across the Harbour on the north shore, near the Malado Cafe where we first met. They are circus people – resting because one of them has an injury. They are gorgeous people and will take care of you there. You won't be far away from me, and you will love the Littlejohn family … but we need a plan.'

'What about the Buchanans,' I asked nervously.

'I will be the go-between with the Buchanans. I will cease paying the rent – no Maria, it's not our problem … but we don't want to let them know what's happening.'

So a plan was hatched. For the next few days I would pack some of my things in a bag and walk to Patricia's car, parked at the end of the road. She would put the bag into her car and take it to Eberhard. This way the Buchanans would not be aware I was leaving. Gradually I would take my things out of the house and disappear.

'Your life is in danger. These people are bad and bad people are bad losers.'

I nodded but I needed money to pay for my little boys keep. 'But I must work Eberhard.'

Eberhard replied softly. 'Yes, I know. You are honest and caring and you do it so beautifully. You want to help people – you want to save everyone. Well what about that government job with the Corrective Services? The one working with women who have committed crimes. You are just learning about life, and it seems it might be a good job-fit for you.'

Eberhard was correct about the jobs - working with people began to give me confidence and for the first time in my life I felt productive – and he was also right about the Littlejohn family – they were kind and welcoming. I often watched the dainty Mrs Littlejohn rehearse – but I still felt unwell. I was a picky eater, very under-nourished and anxious. The Littlejohns were supportive and sang sweet little songs to me. I learned to sing again with them like I would have if I'd have been a little girl who played games – but I was never a little girl. I didn't know how to be a little girl. I had never played games.

When I think back, I know that I had my own way of getting through life; it was to have a palace with many rooms in my mind. I could go to any room and have nice memories – a place for nice times. I could shut out the bad times, I knew my children were safe and I could sleep at night. The Buchanans had given my second little girl to The Salvation Army, but I hadn't forgotten her – I could still see her little face and often thought about her – and, although I thought lovingly of my daughter Michele, she was not the same; living with the Buchanans had already changed her. They didn't know where the boys were, and I knew they weren't interested as they had never wanted the boys anyway.

Eberhard had showed me his loving nature and found a home for the boys where they would be cared for, and I paid for their board. I could visit them in Newcastle, outside Sydney - somewhere nobody would check - in a home run by the United Protestant Association (UPA). My sons were together, and safe (or so I thought). The UPA were one of the few organisations where I could visit my boys. I didn't trust The Salvation Army, I had no faith in the Catholic homes (Catholics hadn't helped me growing up) and, like the welfare people, all the homes would have split up my family and I would be unable to see them. This way I could visit and hug each one to me. As a child, I don't remember ever being hugged so I tried to hug my children when I saw them - but awful mistakes were made. It was not possible to predict what would happen.

* * *

Mentally I went backwards for a while, down into the depths of hopelessness. I was in a bad way when Eberhard decided that seeing my boys would be good for me. He arrived one Saturday morning; I wasn't feeling well but he was positive and coaxed me into going.

'You are going to visit your boys in my car. We will drive steadily - over the river on the Hawkesbury Bridge and through some pretty countryside. You'll feel happier when you've seen the boys.'

I didn't really want to leave the Littlejohns' safe house and felt very nervous. In my mind I sort-of trusted Eberhard and Patricia but I could never really be sure – completely sure. I sat in the passenger seat and watched the river pass underneath, as we drove over the Hawksbury Bridge, and Eberhard drove his car north. Somehow I didn't feel well – not comfortable, not at ease - and to distract myself, I tried to concentrate on the scenery.

I turned back to see the view out the windows, to check the small boats moored on the river and, in shock, saw my evil-looking father was sat in the backseat, staring at me. I clutched Eberhard's arm.

'My father – he's sitting in the back,' I gasped in fright. 'He's in the back, Eberhard.'

Eberhard stayed calm. 'No Maria. Look around you Liebchen, there's nobody there.'

Slowly I turned around and, in terror, said 'Yes, he's there.'

'No' Eberhard said firmly.' It's in your mind. Hold my hand.'

As suggested, I took his free hand and he continued, 'Now repeat after me – 'my father is not in this car'.'

I looked out the window in despair as his fingers pressured me, reminding me what I had to do.

I repeated, 'My father is not in this car.'

Eberhard's calm voice continued to guide me. 'We're climbing up the hill now – look around again Maria. He's not there.'

I noticed outside the car the traffic had become heavier. The woodland scenery slid by, and it took an enormous effort to make my head turn to look at the car's back seat. My father had gone.

'He's gone now – he's not there Maria, is he?' Eberhard's voice, low and composed, brought me back to the present.

I agreed he wasn't there … he had gone.

'You were frightened, and your mind put him in the backseat, but it was only in your mind, Maria. He wasn't really there.'

I still felt agitated and a little terrified, and Eberhard must have noticed. He said 'I'm going to sing to you. Sit back and relax.' Eberhard had often sung and strummed his guitar to me when I was ill. It seemed to sooth me.

'This song was written for my Maria,' Eberhard said quietly and, as he drove along, he softly sang the popular song, 'Rose Marie.'

I sat back in the car and listened to the lyrics. Each tender word resonated with me. I hadn't heard anything as charming and it calmed me down enough to have my first Newcastle visit with my sons. We had a wonderful reunion, and I could see the boys were happy at that stage - the boys weren't faking it. Neither Eberhard nor I saw anything but contented boys with smiling faces, with no bruises on them. We returned to Sydney assuming the boys were in a safe place.

However, years later the UPA recognised the trauma their so-called Christian workers had caused to my boys. Three UPA representatives and a lawyer came to a meeting at the Tweed Ultima Apartments, Gold Coast, where they gave my sons and me thousands of dollars. There, in a room in the Bay Street resort, it was offered as 'shut-up' money. As a grown-up, my middle son never recovered mentally from what he had been exposed to at the hands of paedophiles and suffered for years before dying – no amount of money could make up for that. It showed me what people could get away with under the cloak of religion and how others hushed up the afflicted abuse. It was only the beginning. To stay quiet, the UPA paid many more thousands of dollars to my sons in later years.

* * *

The family's latest threatening behaviour, and trying put distance between me and the Buchanans, had left me in a dreadfully fragile state of mind. I felt I'd never be free, but my friends were still in my life. Vera thought I should be dancing – expressing myself through dance.

'You are a born dancer. You shouldn't be working in the field of pain. You cannot change the world. Your world is music and dance.'

It was true – I only felt free when I lost myself in dance. I worked in many fields – not just to earn a living but to learn about people – but I still felt a little controlled, even though I knew Eberhard was the kindest, most caring man who only wanted the best for me, wanting nothing in return. He wished to see me living a confident and happy life and he eventually wanted to make me his wife and to care for my children – he was always so sweet with them – but I couldn't completely trust him. I only ever wanted him as a friend. Actually, I couldn't completely trust anyone – not Eberhard, not the sweet Patricia, not Vera, not Tess, not even the wonderful Littlejohns. Each of them thought I was free of the mind-control my family, and the Buchanans, had put me through but I knew I had not completely broken-free – old habits die hard. All my childhood I had been strictly controlled and none of them completely understood.

Brainwashing is said to reduce its subjects' ability to think critically or independently. I had to allow new thoughts and ideas into my mind, as well as to change my attitude and belief – to over-print the family's ideas with my own new viewpoint. Each time I made progress it was reversed by the continued menacing from my family and the close proximity of Mrs Buchanan, reinforcing their original mind-set. Without actually meaning to, I still looked for my mother's, father's or Lyall's faces in crowds, evil people who could band together and destroy me. I was in limbo – a nice limbo, surrounded by adorable people; I had so much kindness, and support – but it was all too much. I felt overwhelmed.

Life went on and, trying to get back on track, I decided I wanted to live on my own – to see if I could live as an adult without the continual visits from Eberhard and Patricia. I didn't want to live or even share with anyone or be under their constant protection. After all, Patricia lived on her own as did Eberhard. I informed them both, 'I want to make my own decisions and not discuss every move with you. I don't want you to come over every evening to see if I'm coping.'

I still looked under-nourished. I didn't eat much and continued the doctor's visits, unaware that cancer had begun in my body, but I had fond memories of the boy's happy smiling faces – I was unaware what was happening to them – and knew I was returning.

By now I was employed in the New South Wales Corrective Services. I had trained at Longbay Prison and worked with women prisoners at Silverwater Prison. I treated all the inmates as human beings – like I would wish to have been treated if I were in their circumstances. In my blue prison uniform I earned their respect as I handled them all the same. I still wanted to help people – the powerless, unworldly, and down-trodden – but corners were being cut and I didn't want to cut corners. I wanted to carry out my duties without being cruel or condescending.

The biggest shock came when dealing with the women prisoners – some were nice ordinary mothers, some should really not have been in there. I worked amongst people with addictions and people of cultures, and I handled them all the same. I was to see more horror in the many jobs I worked and never understood what made people act the way they did. I saw how a few prisoners became powerful figures who enforced their influence over the others and also how guards acted towards prisoners. When given power, something happens to some people, and they become dominant. Watching cruelty inflicted and not doing anything about it is wrong.

Later on, when I moved to Brisbane, I went into Wacol Prison with the Victims' Module – prisoners who had committed crimes against children. Most expressed no regrets except to get caught. One prisoner turned to me and told me I was tough - 'tough enough to rust.' Now I am a speaker as a survivor – not a victim. I have proved I'm a survivor – I didn't die. I came out of a world where I had no love, no control in any way, not even a birthdate - until I was told by the doctor at thirteen - and I had worked hard with no pay. Now I worked and received money and, deep down, I was anxious to be my own person.

* * *

Gradually I was beginning to become a person - a whole new person. Something was happening inside of me that even I didn't understand - but it slowly dawned on me that I had started to think for myself, and I still felt under the control of others. Of course, this was now in a nice way rather than the brutality of my family life. Their help came from feelings of friendship – Eberhard, Patricia, Tess, Frau Metchler – all had helped me learn about life, but they were still there in the background, picking up the pieces as I began to open my mind to the real world. I was still controlled by others.

The doctor had told me I had a very good brain, but it had been conditioned by my early experiences. I had to retrain my thinking to accept and evaluate other ideas and delete the older thinking – the conditioned thinking.

I felt confident that I had proved myself capable of making decisions. For instance I could never watch cruelty and stay silent. I wanted only to work where I could assist. I knew that in the nursing homes where I'd worked, even the very sickest people showed they recognised kindness and gentleness. I had reported callousness as I couldn't stand by and see people being cruel to others who had no power. I had proved myself as a prison warder, by not displaying prejudice as I did my duty, that I was the same nature at home as when I worked in my blue prison uniform.

But I had so many secrets, I felt trapped ... I dared not tell everything. I felt I had to take full responsibility for being constantly aware of the havoc the Buchanans and my family could inflict on me or my children at any time. At any moment they could be round the corner in a car – waiting to snatch me back, or worse. The fear was always with me.

Not knowing the entire background, my friends could never understand my insistence that the police were not to be contacted. They could never understand that, as my family were known to the police, I was still part of that family and would not be taken seriously. My friends acted within the law and didn't understand the twisted and brutal way my family would react, or the 'code of silence' that prevented me telling them the full story. I was a commodity to my family, the Buchanans and Tony - Lyall had a wife, his mother had a servant, as did Tony. I was not like the everyday person. There was nothing I could do legally; I knew that if it were ever to come to court, everything that had happened to 'Little Mary' would be explained away. In a courtroom, in my experience, the under-dog seldom wins, and I knew I could have easily ended up being incarcerated in a 'loony bin,' with my children distributed amongst anyone who volunteered to take them. Yes, I had these fears.

I knew I had behaviour patterns which weren't normal. I kept my emotions under wrap – not showing pain or fear or letting my suffering show. From a young child I had been conditioned not to show these feelings – to act as though everything was fine. Any sign of pain and I would receive even more torment, hence my wanting to stop cruelty wherever I had worked - to make things right that were wrong.

All my friends were terribly kind and had done their best to show me how the real world worked. Frau Metchler had built a restaurant in Sydney called The Parisian Pussy Cat. One day she said, 'Gypsy, I want to take you with me to see the restaurant and the staff. I want you to learn about life – about business.'

I didn't see what she thought I would learn but accompanied her anyway. She pointed out the large garbage bins out the back of the building.

'Very important, those bins. In my business, Gypsy, you have to see that the kitchen is always clean, and the staff don't steal.'

I nodded as she continued.

'Now, you see the chef - he finishes his shift at four - in an hour. It's three o'clock and he's just taken a chicken out of the fridge, wrapped it in paper and put it in the garbage bin, which is quite full. Now I know that anything he takes out the fridge, an hour before he leaves, is going to be his. He'll pick up my wrapped chicken, from the top of the garbage bin, on his way out, and he'll cook his chicken at his home. Now that's stealing. I don't mind being asked for help, but no-one steals from me.'

I learned another lesson. I was learning to think and be aware that there are people who do horrible things to each other. I was learning about things I had never before thought about.

* * *

CHAPTER 8

DIVORCE

'What would I have to do to get a divorce,' I asked pensively; that question had been on my mind lately. Everyone around me came to a sudden halt. They stopped talking and stared at me. It was Saturday afternoon, and we were just sitting around, chatting, and having tea at the Littlejohn's house – me, Eberhard, Patricia, and Tess. They all blinked and seemed stunned.

'What would I have to do to get a divorce?' I repeated.

'At last' Patricia blurted out with excitement.

Eberhard looked at me and said softly 'You are a brave girl. It's so good to see you making your own decisions. You're beginning to realise you are free.'

I smiled but I knew I wasn't free. I might not be living with them, but I wasn't free of the family. They wouldn't let me go, just like that, but … it might be different if I had a divorce. Now, I didn't truly know what the word meant other than I would be no longer married to Lyall. When I asked how it would affect my children's future, I found that Patricia had already started the ball rolling. She had been in contact with a solicitor and discussed the over-all path in gaining custody of my children when divorcing. She warned me it would be a long process - there would be multiple visits to the solicitor's office and many documents to sign before the divorce case could be placed before a judge.

I told my friends I wanted to think about it and, again wishing to take charge of my own life, I decided to visit my daughter Michele without telling anyone. *I'm thinking for myself now and making my own decisions and I want to see my daughter. I want to see Michele.*

Without telling anyone, I made my way to my previous address. The Buchanans must have been paying rent as they were still living in the house Eberhard had set up for me. I knocked at the door, and it was opened by Mrs Buchanan. One look at her face, showed me that I wasn't welcome, and in that split second, I thought that maybe I had made a mistake. *Perhaps I should have told Eberhard and Patricia what I'd planned to do.* I didn't get past the doorstep; she didn't invite me in.

'What do you want?' Mrs Buchanan thundered, sneering at me.

'I've come to see my daughter.'

'No' Mrs Buchanan bellowed, moving her head back and forth in denial. 'She's Lyall's daughter, not your daughter.'

My stomach churned as I replied '… but I gave birth to her in hospital. She's my daughter.'

Probably hearing the clamour at the door, little Michele appeared at Mrs Buchanans side.

'Hello, my darling' I said quietly and smiling, I put out my arms for her. She looked back blankly, unsmiling, and replied 'Hello.' She didn't move forward towards me and my heart broke as she turned round, disinterested, and went back inside. Mrs Buchanan continued to yell menacingly.

'If you want your girl, you'd better get back to your husband.'

I stared back at her and, for the very first time, stood up for myself. I straightened up and tried to sound firm as I shook my head and said, 'I'm not going back.'

Mrs Buchanan sniffed. 'You'll go back – now get out of here,' she snarled. I stood my ground on the doorstep, staring her back as she continued ranting. 'If you try to divorce my son, we have ways to prove she's not yours. You don't stand a chance. Now, I told you, get out of here.'

I left and returned to the Littlejohn's where I confessed what I had done. They were stunned and told me it had been an awful mistake – like stepping into the lion's den. I knew I should have discussed it with them, but I had so wanted to see Michele.

'They're now warned you're becoming stronger and thinking of the next step - going for a divorce. They'll find out where you live.'

I shrugged, knowing I had been followed many times. 'But they know everything – where I live – who I see – everything.'

As it turned out, the divorce wasn't the big problem we had all expected. I visited the solicitor's office with Eberhard and Patricia and found they had organised the preparatory work and the solicitor told me I had taken very wise steps to protect myself and my children. There were numerous papers to sign, and he said he did not expect any problems unless my husband decided to fight it. My insides tightened up, but the solicitor seemed quite confident.

'I don't honestly think he's stupid enough to fight this so don't worry.'

He was right. The day arrived and Eberhard was smiling and happy. 'Pipkin, you are soon going to be free. The solicitor is not afraid. There has been no sign from the Buchanan family that they will be there in court.'

In the end the split was uncontested, and it went through – I was granted a divorce and the magistrate awarded me full custody of the children. No-one from my past turned up, not Lyall, not any of them.

'I knew he wasn't going to contest' a beaming Eberhard said. 'Lyall couldn't stand up in court. He would have ended up in jail. You're a free woman now.'

Butterflies were flying back and forth in my stomach and I smiled and repeated 'Yes - I'm free.' Actually it didn't sink in that I was free for some time, but I did feel I'd had 'a win' even though I didn't understand what 'win' actually was or what 'being free' would really mean for me.

'Did you understand it all?' Eberhard gently asked on the way home from the court.

'Yes,' I replied. 'When the final papers are issued, I will no longer be married to Lyall, and the children are under my custody. That means I can go and get Michele back.'

Eberhard hesitated a moment or two. 'Mmm, well yes, but slow down. It wouldn't be fair to Michele to go rushing round to scoop her up, Maria. Not just yet. You have to think about the child's feelings. Don't push her.'

I was anxious to collect her from the Buchanans, but I agreed that I would have to take Michele's feelings into consideration and not rush to collect her. We went back to Frau Metchler's house for afternoon tea and there were so many people waiting. Everyone I knew was there and they all clapped me when they heard Eberhard announce the news. After the general chatter, Eberhard took me by the hand and led me into the centre of the crowd, and they made a circle around us. In front of everybody, he knelt down on one knee before me, and the room went quiet. They stood watching as he said 'Will you marry me, Maria? I want to care and cherish you. I love you and your little children who are part of you. Will you be my wife?'

No … no… I thought. Marry … marry Eberhard? I want to be free … leave me be, I don't want to be a wife to anyone, belong to anyone … but … how can I stop this - in front of all these people … how can I say no? Bewildered, I knew I could not refuse, and murmured 'Yes.'

From his pocket, Eberhard took out a ring and placed it on my finger - we were engaged. Everyone gathered round and congratulated us. I smiled and nodded but later, when we were alone Eberhard could see I wasn't thrilled and asked me how I was feeling.

'Um … really Eberhard, well … I don't really want to be married.'

Eberhard smiled and tried to reassure me. 'Maria, it's not going to be like your last marriage. I want to love and protect you - and the children. I want you to be happy. I promise I won't force you to do anything against your will. I only want to bring you happiness.'

It was a lot to take in – *in one day I have been granted a divorce and custody of my children, been proposed to, and now I'm engaged to be married to Eberhard.* I knew I needed to learn to get on with life, living like normal people and be free of the past – but I couldn't get over the fact that Lyall and the family had stayed quiet – too quiet. But I had to stop being afraid.

Why would they want me now? I don't belong to Lyall anymore – I'm no longer his slave. I really must lock up my painful past and stop being afraid. I have to try to be the person my friends say I am.

* * *

I continued to live at the Littlejohn's home, learning new things about life, doing lots of small jobs, but I knew I felt I had to stop the world being a bad place for some. I was aware I had this impulse to find fault and I was still unsure about being married again. I was happy being with Eberhard - but marriage? *I've been married to that weak sick man who gambled his money and gave me away to pay his debts. Do I want to take a risk with Eberhard?*

Just as I felt things were going well, something would come along to change things. Out of the blue, as I walked near home one day, my ex-husband Lyall appeared. He had obviously waited to surprise me and said 'Hello Mary. Remember me?'

I stood stock still, glued to the spot - dumbfounded.

'Don't talk to me. I don't want anything to do with you,' I stammered.

'I just want to talk Mary. You won't call the police, will you? … I've been looking for you … look, everything … all the problems … it's not me, it was Mum – she rules the roost.'

I couldn't move away. I no longer felt afraid of him but was spellbound, looking at this skinny, ugly man who I had allowed to bully to me for all those years.

He continued, 'Mary, I made a big mistake with you. I want you back as my wife. Mum ruined everything – for me, even for Joyce. She's got no husband because of Mum. Mary, I want you back.'

I stared coldly back at him and said steadfastly, 'I'm not your wife.'

'Mary, I want you back. It's not that I'm not getting 'any' either. I drive women to and from the cigarette factory and many of the women would rather not pay the fare in cash. They give me what I need, but I want you back.'

My stomach was churning over, but I remained strong. 'I'm divorced,' I spluttered, trying to make him understand.

'… but Mary, I want you back.'

I was able to get one word out before I turned and walked away shouting 'No.' Putting one foot in front of the other, I made my way down the street, Lyall calling after me - 'Mary. Mary.' The sound echoed and was the only thing I could hear as I walked away.

By the time Eberhard and Patricia visited me later, I had composed myself but was still shaken-up. They could see all was not well and wanted to know what had happened to upset me so. They were outraged when I explained what had happened. Patricia wanted to call the police, but Eberhard said 'Just try not to think about it. There is Michele to consider.'

He was right. Eberhard suggested I make contact with Michele but not insist she come to live with me, so slowly I did, and she came to stay for a night at first, then later, a weekend. She seemed happy to be with us but wanted to go back to the Buchanan's after a couple of days and that became the pattern for us for years to come – that odd Buchanan family had some sort of hold over her. She was never truly happy there but became uncomfortable staying with me. She knew I loved her, but she grew up to become footloose and unsettled.

Around this time, I had another visit from one of my father's henchmen. Going to my car after work, an Italian man approached and asked me if the grey car was mine. When I nodded, he aggressively told me my father wanted to see me. I refused and his parting words were 'You WILL see him, Mary Goodfield … he doesn't want to hurt you, but he wants you to go to the Chullora house.'

I shrugged and got into my car determined not to even think about it, but later I told Eberhard and he felt I should go - but only if he accompanied me - for my safety.

That was how I found myself, a few days later, at my parents old house, knocking on the back door. I had dressed neatly, and Eberhard was beside me in a smart get-up with a cravat at his neck. My father opened the door and seemed slightly taken aback to see me with the smartly dressed Eberhard. We were not invited into the house and spoke on the back-door steps.

My father, in his usual bow tie, noted I had brought 'the Bavarian' with me, and told me he wanted me to go to a family meeting in Melbourne with Violet's son (my half-brother who was a senior crime figure there). He and my mother would be driving there and wanted me there too. My confidence was quite boosted with Eberhard standing next to me, so I made no comment and didn't cave in straight away. However, after my father pressured me to confirm, reluctantly, I agreed to go to Melbourne. In a menacing voice, the last thing he said was, 'You'd better keep your promise, Mary.'

* * *

I still wonder if my family had a malicious plan - an ulterior motive - to get me to Melbourne, but I will never know. On the way to Melbourne, my parents were involved in a dreadful car crash in Yass, just some seven hours from Melbourne. My father was killed, and my mother seriously injured. No-one in the family wanted to identify my father's body so it was left to me to drive to the Yass police station. In the mortuary, I saw his cold dark eyes were finally closed for good. When I looked at his blood-stained face, I felt nothing, but I knew I'd seen the devil. To myself I thought *huh, I kept my promise – Yass is almost Melbourne.* My mother had survived but lost sight in one eye and had many other serious injuries which hospitalised her for months.

For the time being, my boys stayed in the UPA home and Michele visited but lived with the Buchanans. Eventually Eberhard and I talked about marrying. He wanted to give me the full bridal experience but, despite us both being born into the Catholic Church, knew I felt it had let me down. He also had been unhappy with the Catholic Church back in Munich so suggested we look at the Greek Orthodox Church.

'A friend of mine, who I work with, is Greek and talks highly of his church and a priest named Elladios Zoghaphakis. I thought we might go and have a look at his Greek Orthodox Church and meet this priest.'

I must have looked doubtful as he continued to speak with passion. 'Maria, I want to marry you in a church – you weren't married to Lyall, you were bonded. You deserve to be a bride. I don't know how you feel but since we can't marry in a Catholic church ... well ... the Greek Orthodox Church doesn't think of divorce in same way as the Catholics.'

This was a new barrier to me, I'd forgotten ... *of course, as a divorced woman, I can't marry Eberhard in a Catholic church – not that I want to think about marrying again.*

Patricia thought It a beautiful idea and was all for it. 'I heard they have a lot of ceremony in their church. Greek people here don't seem to be troubled and get into crime like some others. They're very family minded.' Seeing my hesitant response, Patricia continued, 'I'm on Eberhard's side.'

I knew nothing about the Greek Orthodox Church and agreed to go with him the following week, but despite feeling healthier and putting on weight, I didn't feel ready to be married again. At my regular doctor's appointment I sat opposite the doctor at his desk and asked him if I was healthy now.

'No. You are still seriously undernourished and, having been mentally destroyed, I think there are long-term problems which will show in the future However, I see you are walking upright and with confidence and mentally you have made great strides. Are you eating better?'

I shrugged 'not really.'

Dr Stulzman continued on, telling me to make more of an effort to eat as he didn't think the nutritious injections were needed now.

I plucked up courage and asked, 'What about marriage?'

He was silent for a moment or two. 'Ah … Eberhard,' he said and stopped talking for a moment. Across the desk he nodded and continued, 'Yes, now he is a lovely man, on a par with my own son…reliable, honest, and safe. Of all people, you need to feel safe, Maria. Eberhard will make you feel safe.'

* * *

When the day finally arrived to visit the Greek church, Eberhard picked me up and seemed particularly light-hearted.

As we drove along, he said 'I want to marry you Maria, but with your consent. I don't want to force you, I want you to feel safe. I want us both to look at the church and see how we feel about the Greek religion. I've seen photos of this priest – he has a goatee beard.' He tried his best to make conversation and make me feel comfortable – like we were just going out for the day.

We made our way to Marrickville, and drove past the white St Nicholas Greek Orthodox Church, a breath-taking designed building with arching bell towers at the top of a flights of wide stairs. We parked the car in the large empty carpark, and in awe, climbed the magnificent steps fanning out before the entrance, until we reached the massive church doors. They were open and we peeped inside.

We stood in awe as we took in the sight before us. An enormous chandelier adorned with candles hung above us. The walls were covered from floor to ceiling with bright icons and wall paintings of saints, and stories from the Bible. It was a scene of flashing gold and vivid colours and took my breath away. I felt tight in my chest and emotional – a feeling I'd never had before - and Eberhard seemed similarly overwhelmed. In silence, we sat down on some nearby seats and continued to try to take in the opulence of the church. After a while Eberhard took my hand and we walked back to the main entrance, where a priest came to meet us. The man had a goatee beard and looked just like the images of God I'd known as a child. He informed us his name was Elladios Zoghaphakis.

Eberhard introduced me and himself and explained he had asked me to be his wife but we both brought up in the Catholic church and had bad experiences. 'Your church is quite beautiful,' he added.

The priest replied, 'The people have made it so. They've put part of themselves into the building.'

Eberhard explained we wanted to be married in a church and were interested in learning about the Greek Orthodox religion. The priest invited us into his office and asked why we both wished to learn. Eberhard became very serious as he spoke. 'With Maria's permission I will tell you a little of her life.' He revealed everything he knew including how I was sold into marriage. Elladios Zoghaphakis replied that it's not a marriage if you are sold into it and, in a sympathetic gesture, leaned over and took my hand in his.

Even today, over sixty years later, I remember the feeling – it was though I was standing on a cliff ledge about to slip over into the abyss and a hand - this priest's hand - pulled me back to safety.

'Maria, are you going to accept this man's hand in marriage.'

In a daze I answered 'Yes.'

'… and you want to learn about our faith?'

I nodded. 'Yes, we both want to learn.'

Elladios Zoghaphakis nodded too. 'I will teach you. We do not change our religion to please man. We cannot change what is written down. If you come here one night a week, I will teach you everything.'

Eberhard and I returned to the car without speaking a word. We both felt meeting Elladios Zoghaphakis had been an incredible experience; in a reflective mood, we drove back. On arrival at the Littlejohn's, Eberhard had tears in his eyes as he said 'Maria, I promise I will care for you as long as I breath – and even after I stop breathing, I will look after you. Let's speak about this tomorrow. I think we should sleep on it. Tomorrow we will talk, talk honestly and truthfully – make a vow about what we feel.'

After he left, I busied myself making tea then sat doing nothing for a couple of hours, just contemplating the impression that sitting in the church and talking to the priest had me feel.

Next day arrived and I asked myself what I was going to say to Eberhard? *Can I put the horrors of my life as Mary, with my family and the Buchanans, behind me? Can I trust Eberhard, a man seven years younger than me, to protect me like an older man would? Could he teach me the things I should already know – my rights, the ways of the world and how to be happy? Now I am Maria, I have to decide.*

Physically I had put on a little weight and people now said I was a beautiful woman but that was just the outer layer – on the inside, this thirty-nine-year-old woman was just a very inexperienced girl, reliant on others to teach her things. I had gradually come to terms with my agoraphobia and claustrophobia – both still affected me from time to time, but it was mostly under my control. I never set out to hurt anyone, and I didn't understand cruelty in others. I knew that I kept trying to change the entire world. I had to accept that my small acts of kindness could only make a small difference and there will always be cruelty in the world.

When Eberhard arrived, we thrashed out what we had thought of the Greek Orthodox Church and the priest – was it good, bad, or just all right. I didn't say I thought I'd been touched by the hand of God in case Eberhard thought I was mad. But when he asked if I felt we had a future together, my reply was 'Yes.' I agreed to put the previous horrors behind me and take the risk.

* * *

Over the next twelve months, we spent one night each week with Elladios Zoghaphakis and learned about the religion. It emphasized we are all equal before God (shown in the church by standing equal distance from the altar), and that men are not superior to women and the religion went back many hundreds of years without change. Soon we became part of the Greek congregation who adopted us new followers into their flock and were most welcoming. The offers of assistance for our marriage ceremony were numerous as the locals gathered around us. Nick and Tess Adams were to be our ceremony sponsors and were very well-known businesspeople in the community. They had many contacts, and through them my beautiful lace wedding dress was made and gifted, as well as a five-tier iced wedding cake. We were even offered a honeymoon in Greece but were unable to take it as the boys were, by now, living with me – they were to take part in the ceremony, carrying candles.

The night before the wedding, I stayed with girlfriends, preparing for the next day. Around midnight, I became aware of a commotion outside the house and found everyone looking out the window. In the street below, Eberhard serenaded me in a magnificent singing voice. His friend Franco, who sang off-key, helped him sing beautiful love songs to me. I wasn't actually allowed near the window, being told it was bad luck for the groom to see the bride the night before a wedding. The whole street could have complained about being woken but I found it to be a most touching offering by my darling prince charming and I went to bed smiling.

Approaching the church next day, the sun shone down on the magnificent wedding car I was travelling in, as it wound its way slowly along. To my amazement I saw my daughter Michele, now a teenager, standing on the pavement near the church entrance and I ordered the chauffeur to stop. Michele looked into the wedding car and saw me, and I wound the window down to speak to her. Her smiling face came near.

'I so wanted to see you on your special day … you look lovely,' she whispered sweetly. I felt splendid in the wonderful lace gown, with my hair and nails glowing in the sunlight.

'Please come to the church – to the wedding. You know I want you there.' I replied, my heart filled with love.

Michele stepped back and shook her head. 'No .. I love you, but I won't – I just wanted to see you.'

I felt so sad as I entreated, 'I'd love you to be there Michele.'

'I know you care' she said 'but I won't come. You look so lovely – really lovely.' She turned and walked away, and the car carried on to the church where all my new friends waited.

In the church, my eldest son stood with the Best Man, and the two younger boys carried tall candles. In my wonderful lace dress, I felt as if I was floating. It was an ancient religious ceremony where, a single ribbon was attached to two crowns, called Stefana. Together, the priest placed them on our heads, a symbol that we were crowned by God as king and queen of our home and founders of a new generation. The crowns were exchanged on our heads three times by our sponsors, Nick, and Tess, who gifted us newlyweds a silver tray on the wedding table to hold our crowns and rings.

During the ceremony, the priest joined our right hands as he called upon God to unify us into one mind and body. Prayers were said for a long and peaceful life of health and happiness. Our hands remained joined throughout the service to show our union - a touching and meaningful ceremony, surrounded by my sons and our friends. The ceremony was such an emotional moment. I was thirty-nine and it was nothing at all like the lonely, dispassionate Baptist church service I had gone through with Lyall at seventeen.

* * *

CHAPTER 9

LIFE WITH EBERHARD

I suppose, dear readers, you would think that, with a kind, caring and attentive husband, my dreams had come true, but I was too busy learning how to deal with this new life. Not only did I have to think about myself and my children, now there was also Eberhard. My work doubled as I learned to live as a married woman with a house and a family of five to manage, and also work in the Granville factory Eberhard owned.

We lived in a house he had bought in the same area, so suddenly, my workload increased as I performed a full-time job and had a household and a family to care for, plus in the evenings, I became Attara. My dancing was much in demand and brought in a large amount of money. Eberhard took great pride in accompanying me to these jobs, driving me to and fro – a devoted, helpful husband; whilst my new husband held my chair for me and opened doors, he never once picked up a plate or helped with the washing-up.

My bad health, from years of abuse, didn't relieve my feelings of discontent. Living on my own, I had worked during the day, ignoring the discomfort, and struggled with pain through the night. Now Eberhard was there, I had to keep it all under wraps – I had no outlet for my pain and the illness took hold as I suffered in silence.

I had even less time to think about my own woes as my mother

Violet, was transferred to Sydney's Bankstown Hospital, and I cooked and took her food since she refused to eat what the hospital offered.

I had always wanted a mother's love and found myself still seeking my mother's approval (which I never received – not even a 'sorry' for my horrific childhood.) Violet recovered enough to return to her life, but now with a limp and the loss of sight in one eye. I soon found I was trapped between what I was afraid of (somehow, I was still afraid of her – old habits die hard), and what I wanted her to be. Violet was still a powerhouse, a manipulating, evil lady with a lot of money who often called me, on the landline phone in the middle of the night, to rush to her side for some imagined drama, still showing her control. Likewise, I continued to seek her love and approval, both of which she still denied me.

Eventually she sought out someone who she could completely dominate. She found a slightly backward, dull man who, repeating her marriage pattern, became her domestic slave. She happily allowed him to take care of her money and clean her jewellery – 'A clever man will take everything and leave you, but a dullard stays and cares.' - he did.

After a long illness, and pleas to her sons and their wives to care for her (which they ignored), I was the one who visited her and took her meals up until her death. Because she didn't like her daughters-in-law, she told me 'I don't want the boys to take my jewellery and have their wives wear them. They can't have them, and I don't want any of them here when I go.' She gave Eberhard a white purse, inside were a bunch of pawn tickets. She had taken her jewels to a pawn shop and pawned them for a pittance. If I wanted them, I had to redeem them from the pawn shop – in this way there was no way my family could contest her giving them to me. (I checked this with her solicitor who agreed this was legal and could not be contested.)

She was cunning my mother Violet Jesse, and she had some beautiful jewellery. I recall as a child, accompanying her to a small jeweller's shop in a side street in Paddington to buy diamonds. Both Tilly Devine and Kate Leigh, who were known for their rings, vied with each other in showing off their diamonds from their ill-gotten gains and my mother did the same. So when she gave me the purse, it was more through her dislike of her sons' wives than any kindness to me. She certainly never gave me love which was free. She died in hospital after a stroke.

When I did redeem the diamonds, I left a few small ones in the purse which I dropped into my mother's grave at the burial. My brothers watched in horror and, from then on, always suggested I stole their inheritance. Actually I sold the remaining jewellery and distributed the money to help people who were in need. One of them was my middle son who was ill with lung problems. I replaced the furniture and whitegoods in the apartment he shared with his girlfriend. The remainder of the jewellery money went to the Gold Coast people I was trying to help – the homeless, the poor, and the charities who helped these people.

With both my parents dead, I had to think for myself. I felt at peace, able to lay the past to rest, however, I began to feel guilty that I wasn't as overwhelmed with happiness as I should have been. I had freedom and power as a housewife, being married to this wonderful man, who was so good with my children, but I gradually noticed chinks began to appear in Eberhard's 'armour.' He started to act a little odd - just small things. I felt he saw me as a young, pretty trophy he was proud of, but I attracted all the attention, and he did not. I felt he was uncomfortable with this and even Patricia noticed and told me she thought Eberhard was becoming a little jealous of my limelight.

Eberhard handled all the money, my wages as well as the lucrative evening, dancing income, and I accepted our way of life … until he informed me he was returning to Germany for a short time, to see his mother who was in ill health. It peeved me that he never wanted me to go with him – in fact, he returned to Germany several times over the years, and not once did he suggest

I accompany him - his new Australian wife - to meet his German family … I had to wonder why.

He knew I would cope alone in Sydney, and he returned within a few weeks, telling me about the family reunion with his mother, brother, and sister, who had married an extremely rich man, and they had a daughter.

About this time Eberhard became a soccer coach with his friend Franco, and they were very successful. Eberhard was called 'Mr Ed' by the dads and featured in the German soccer club's limelight, which he adored. He also had another friend in Sydney named Harry, who he had known in Germany, where they had performed 'The Schuhplattler' a traditional style of folk dancing popular in Southern German. In this dance, the male performers stomp, clap and strike the soles of their shoes, thighs and knees with their hands held flat, making loud slapping noises, having mock-fights and horseplay. The audience thinks the men are fighting but it's all noise and no-one is hurt. It is often interspersed with females dancing basic steps wearing colourful costumes. Harry and Eberhard decided to perform this in Sydney, and I was invited to join.

Whilst Eberhard insisted I dance with the German dance troop, I didn't like this type of dancing. It held no charm for me, consisting of basic movements and Eberhard lifting me up. I much preferred my own Spanish and Moorish dancing where I could release my personality into the performance. After performing the German dance at a club in Sydney's Bayswater Road, Kings Cross, the manager, who had previously seen me dance solo, offered me five hundred pounds to dance a Flamenco solo there, one night a week. When Eberhard turned the offer down, the manager became offended, disclosing what an excellent offer it was since he only paid five hundred pounds a week for a nightly performance by the well-known TV personality, Abagail.

As my boys grew older, like any mother, I wanted to ensure they were safe. Eberhard often complained I over-indulged them.

He said I needed to allow them to make mistakes whilst I tried to ensure they didn't make any. He was probably a little jealous of my time and attention. One year he took my middle son on holiday to Germany with him to stay with his family, and my son enjoyed it so much he didn't want to come back to Australia.

My youngest son decided he wanted to travel on his own and went to Germany, staying with Eberhard's sister and her family. On the driving trip to Italy, a car hit their car, causing serious damage. In the middle of the night, we received a phone call from the Australian police that my son had been in a serious car accident which killed Eberhard's brother-in-law and put his sister, and my son in hospital. The two survivors had been air-lifted to a hospital in Switzerland for treatment as they were so badly injured and needed specialist care. With one relative dead, and my son and his sister Gisela badly injured, Eberhard rushed to Europe.

Now common sense should have told me to go with him to see my injured son, but it was never discussed. Eberhard took charge and, once again, I had no say. Eberhard was in control, and I was not. I didn't think of challenging him and anyway, I had no money to buy an air-ticket and passport.

It proved to me I was still a second-class citizen who fitted in with everybody else so that I didn't cause problems - still looking over my shoulder to the past. I knew my family and Tony were sore losers, still waiting for me to open my mouth and spew out their secrets that, to this day, are not safe for me to tell. In their criminal world I was still theirs and Mary was still tucked away inside me, despite being a celebrity in dancing areas, having the confidence to perform at special events. Deep down I still believed I had no real choice in life.

Eventually my son recovered and returned, as did Eberhard, but I recognised that I had become more and more unimportant in our marriage. Eberhard had never truly treated me as a partner. He had another couple of trips to Germany and again, there was no question of travelling with him. My marriage, which had been a picture of perfection – a beautiful garden full of flawless flowers - now had weeds … and the weeds had started to spread. I hadn't – or didn't want – to notice their taking over.

These days I wonder if Eberhard had begun to change over the years or had he always been so controlling, and we didn't see it. How could I not have seen it – how did Patricia not see it? He had taught me so many wonderful things about life, been so sweet to me, such a lovely person.

I had begun to see less of Patricia whilst I was attending to Eberhard and the children, and she began to prepare to move to another State. I was terribly sad to be losing my friend – we had become more than friends – more like sisters as she had been so caring and wonderful to me. In one of our talks, she told me she hoped, one day, to fall madly in love. 'You know, like you and Eberhard.'

'I suppose so,' I answered, 'sort of.'

'No, not 'sort of,' she interrupted. 'Love is when you have overwhelming respect and trust in a person. Maria, I love you like a sister and would do anything for you. That's love.'

'Yes' I replied, nodding but still unsure. 'I feel the same but I'm not sure I'd describe it as love.'

Patricia continued, 'I will always keep you in my heart Maria – that's love. I also love Eberhard - like a brother. He's a wonderful husband, kind and sweet. Remember how he showed you love and kindness – how he helped you to eat? He's a good man. Maybe he does crave the attention he sees you getting but promise me you will always care for him.'

Now reader, I knew I was living in a fake world, still not free; there were still restraints. When I explained to Patricia how I felt, she was astounded.

'But you are free Maria – you do make decisions and have opinions. Don't let these hidden feelings grow. Discuss this with Eberhard … talk it out.'

Although my solo dancing had become a lucrative side-line and produced a lot of cash, I never saw what happened to the money.

Unlike Lyall, Eberhard gave me plenty of cash for groceries and anything I needed to spend on the house or clothes, but he handled the money and household accounts. As he never went out on his own in the evenings, I had no reason to think he was spending, but I had a nagging feeling I was still being kept in the dark.

One day, near my birthday, as Patricia had suggested, I mentioned as much to Eberhard - that I had no money of my own. He straight away produced a hundred pounds and placed it on the table.

'There you are. Go buy something for your birthday.'

I had learnt that people celebrated birthdays with cake and presents – a new concept to me as I'd grown up in a household where none of that happened - but Eberhard's reaction to my dilemma didn't exactly deal with how I felt. When he found that I had brought things for the boys, he became annoyed and suggested I buy things for myself - things I hankered after – things that I longed for. Actually, I never really yearned for any 'thing' but still there lingered a thought that I harboured – I didn't have a house – not one in my own name. A house of my own spelt the ultimate security to me. Forever in my mind, I still expected one day that my torturers (my brothers or Mrs Buchanan) would, somehow, exact their malicious ways on me – 'leopards don't change their spots.' I had many thoughts that I'd never be completely free of them even though my loving husband would be there to protect me.

People looking at Eberhard and me, saw I was good looking, a gentle, sweet, and obedient wife who didn't stray – everything the average man wanted. I kept a decent household, looked after the family, went to work during the day and had well-paid jobs dancing some nights - and to top it all I had a handsome, charming prince taking care of me. Everyone thought I was living 'happily ever after.' Despite my not realising it, over the years we had become a wealthy couple, with different businesses and buying a few houses. I never questioned whether my name was on the deeds, despite my providing money towards the purchases. I sometimes wondered why

Eberhard never discussed it in depth, but I gave him the benefit of the doubt. I had only received kindness and I trusted him. But I also wondered why he never invited me to travel to Germany on his many trips there. I had begun to think for myself.

* * *

One day Patricia told me she had some information to make me smile.

'Lyall has remarried. He married a woman from the cigarette factory. I'm told she's a very nice person.'

'Poor lady' was all I could say - another life the Buchanans touched.

Patricia cared for Eberhard because he had done so much for me, but she didn't live with us or see that this kind, sweet man was also my keeper. He was an adorable man with an amazing intelligence, able to turn his hand to anything and everything, and he did it to perfection. My beloved Eberhard, my gallant young Bavarian, had actually taught me to trust, to love life, and helped and supported me - but slowly, over the years, he turned into somebody I didn't really know. I found he had faults and I didn't understand them. I had to learn to put aside my feelings and concentrate on the wonderful things he'd done for me in the past when I needed him most. But our marriage was not the fairy-tale people would like to believe – the one with a completely happy ending. I was beginning to think things were not exactly as they should be. Eberhard made all the decisions, and I was expected to agree.

Everyone else thought he was such a wonderful husband. They saw a nice-looking chap, a real gentleman who kissed ladies hands and bowed – Eberhard proved that chivalry was not dead - and women adored him. He was certainly a strong businessman - hard but straight and honest. He never cut corners, paying our bills and taxes, but he held the purse-strings in our marriage. After a while I began to wonder why I didn't ever pay for and own things. – after all, I had also brought a great deal of money in with wages and my lucrative solo dancing. In our marriage, I took it for granted that money was not a worry, but he, and he alone, held the power of the purse-strings. I began to silently question why he had all the control. I had never questioned which bank the money went into or in whose name.

I suppose I still felt like little Mary inside and didn't want to make waves, but silently, I knew my husband was drifting away. I was older than him but looked quite a lot younger – in fact, people often thought he was my father, much to his annoyance. So, I was the trophy on his arm, but he seemed to want to, somehow, out-shine me. His success as a coach at the soccer club made him very proud – he loved the adulation and insisted the success of the German dancing group, which had become a successful dancing group, surpassed my solo dancing (where he didn't receive adoration.)

I had never enjoyed dancing to the German formula dance. I found the music too heavy, I loved the Spanish music which touched my heartstrings. I could express my personality and dancing to it made me feel good … but it held no esteem for him, so was of no interest.

Although we had been married for forty years it was no fairy-tale. I realised that Eberhard thought he'd out-live me when I heard him talking to friends. I'd had a recent breast cancer diagnosis and operation, he told them that there was no real cure – breast cancer always came back.

'People don't live too long after breast cancer,' I heard him say and a chill went through my heart. He obviously didn't expect me to live into old age especially as I'd been hospitalised so often – neck, kidneys, collapsed lung and now cancer. He possibly thought he'd still be a young man and end up with everything anyway – we had both made our Wills, leaving all to each other. I began to notice that he had started to act differently too.

One day I was home, vacuuming and I noticed he'd left his

jacket on the couch which was unlike him. I yanked up the jacket to hang it up and, as I swung it over the couch, a large weight fell out and hit me on the leg. When I picked it up I saw it was a wallet stuffed with money – an enormous roll of cash, about five thousand dollars. Later that night, I asked why he carried such a large roll of money on him, and he went berserk.

'How dare you touch my things? Don't ever touch anything of mine. What right do you have? It's not your right.'

He wasn't interested in my explanation and things were tense between us for a while.

I suppose I was happy most of the time – you only know how happy you are when you look back - but I had started to develop self-confidence – for me it was the vanity of power. People paid to see me dance and I appeared to enjoy the dance display. … and that felt like power. After years of being a slave with no control, I began to believe I should have some say in my life.

I still had fears – mainly about the criminal aspects of my family and their associates, the awful Buchanans – I worried they could make serious trouble. One day a man turned up on our doorstep looking for Mary Buchanan. Both Eberhard and I shook our heads and told him she didn't live there – which was the truth. I had officially divorced and married Eberhard … Eberhard Tinschert, who I began to feel was taking me for granted. Sometimes in these later years, he'd made hurtful, snide remarks. In a marriage understanding and supporting each other is vital but that was now missing. Our marriage became more and more unequal. I had no worldly experience and Eberhard did. If I ever asked 'why' he answered 'that's how things are done. You wouldn't know.'

* * *

We were thinking of selling up and moving house when Eberhard came up with a retirement plan. He felt he had worked on enough Australian Government contracts and had paid enough taxes, that we should try to get something in return. The Government had advertised how small apartments and cottages were provided, at subsidised rents, for older people. Eberhard set out to obtain one in my name. I suppose, since I owned nothing, I fitted the Government's categories, but I wasn't really involved except to sign documents. Eberhard took care of everything, and I received a small housing commission home.

We continued with the sale of our home, and he moved me into this Government place – keeping a unit where he stayed from time-to-time - before going off to Germany to see his family. He was back and forth for some time before he began to look quite ill. We didn't know it then, but he had a cancer growing. He looked very ill and went downhill fast, spending some time in hospital having a stem cell transfer, but it soon became clear the illness was fatal. When the doctor told me they couldn't save him I was devastated.

I was recovering from my first bout of breast cancer but quickly stopped worrying about me to concentrate on Eberhard. I visited every day with the sort of food that he liked, and I listened whilst he complained about everything. One thing irritating him was a nurse with German heritage, who was loud and seemed to feel she had a connection with him. He said he couldn't stand her, and I tried to soothe him by saying there were other nurses, on various shifts, who would be less intrusive.

He had been hospitalised for a couple of months when, one day, a doctor stopped to talk to me about his progress, later as I walked in the hospital corridor I continued on to his room and looked in and stood at the open door in shock. There, before me, lying on the bed with Eberhard was the blonde nurse he had said he so disliked. It was obvious they hadn't been expecting me.

She climbed off the bed smiling and said, 'I suppose I'm going to be involved in a divorce now, am I?' and walked out. Eberhard just looked at me and said nothing. I was stunned to think this hefty nurse thought it acceptable to climb on his bed with him and treat me with contempt when I discovered them. I had spent almost twenty hours each day in the hospital with my dying husband and had been befriended by the regular nurses. When questioned later by these nurses about what had happened, I explained, but declined to pursue it with the hospital authorities – I didn't need any further distractions – but I have never forgotten how that smug woman felt it was acceptable to do that and treat her dying patience's wife that way. From that day I often wondered if he'd been a ladies' man and I just hadn't realised – he'd certainly had plenty of chances and I had never once suspected anything.

He had always been a little controlling about my whereabouts. This showed up when he lay in bed in hospital and he would phone me at home in the morning, wanting to know when I would be in, and also call in the evenings to ensure I was home. Little did I know what lay ahead.

One afternoon as I walked to my car in the hospital car park, I unlocked the door, and a hefty Italian man quickly appeared at my side.

'Hallo Mary' he said in a menacing voice.

With a sinking heart I realised the family nightmare had returned - *he must have been following me. It's starting again.*

'I know all about you and your past. Your friend in Sydney is anxious to know how you are,' he said with a sly smile.

'My past?' I replied. 'My past is long dead – I've been married for a long time.'

He continued on ... 'Lucky I found you. Your dear old friend Tony is concerned about you, and you may soon have more to worry about now that your bodyguard is on the way out. Don't think you should turn your back on old friends - they have a way of turning nasty, your old friends.'

I replied, 'I had no old friends - back then I had no friends.'

He shrugged, spun round, and walked away. I didn't know

what to think. Frightened witless, I realised he knew about Eberhard lying in his hospital bed. I didn't know what to do. I knew I couldn't tell Eberhard at this time, on his death bed. I couldn't tell anyone.

That evening when talking to my son, I told him how tiring I found the driving back and forth to the hospital, after being with Eberhard all day. He offered to do the driving and give me a break. The Italian must have seen me with my son – by now a broad, tall man – and there were no more attempts to talk to me. But it left me in a terrible state, all these years later, still looking over my shoulder. A few weeks later, I drove myself again and after visiting Eberhard, returned to the hospital car park to find a note on the bonnet of my car. The note said 'Hello Mary, still looking good. Can't wait to see you … The Italian Club.'

I nearly collapsed with fright. *The threats will never stop … but I can't have Eberhard see me looking worried. He'll think I've had bad news about his health.*

Next day, back at Eberhard's bedside, I was my usual smiling, concerned self and I stayed that way for every visit. I never understood why Tony would be interested in me at this late stage in both our lives.

* * *

CHAPTER 10

ON MY OWN

During this period I felt terrible sad that I was about to lose Eberhard. He had given me many years of happiness through a loving relationship. I wanted to be there, at his side 24/7, with him in his time of need. As the days went by, when not visiting him in hospital, I tidied up some of his things at home and continually found large rolls of bank notes hidden away. I had no idea why he felt the need to hide cash from me, but his health wasn't improving, and I kept my questions to myself.

When I said goodbye that last evening, and left him in the hospital, I went home to bed with a heavy heart. Eberhard died the next day and I was in his hospital room, holding his cold hand and staring at my dead husband, when the amorous nurse came in. She stared at me and passionately declared, 'I loved him,' and walked out. I was astounded and didn't know what to think. For me, Eberhard's death was an awful tragedy – he was younger than me and, with my bad health, we had both expected me to be the one to die first. As it turned out there were many more shocks to come.

Not long after his funeral I found my beloved Eberhard was preparing to leave me destitute in the little government-owned house. I discovered that, during our forty plus years together, he had put thousands of dollars aside and every property and business in his name. It seems he was preparing to return to Germany with the money and vanish from my life. Never, ever, would I have expected him to do this.

He left me with a heartache which will never go away - his was the ultimate betrayal. All the trust I had built up - since Maria took over from Mary – it all disappeared, everything turned to dust.

My anger intensified as I discovered that, over the years, Eberhard had turned into a scheming two-timer, with money skilfully hidden in even more and more places. Though he hid our money from me, he wasn't quite as clever as he thought. Because he considered himself invincible, he'd forgotten one of the basics – he forgot to change his Will. That oversight left me, his wife Maria Tinschert, the sole beneficiary.

Despite my bad health I continued to work, attending to people - doing what I could to give them love and kindness. In turn, they made me feel appreciated. Over the years, among other professions, I have been a Jenny Craig councillor, and a community carer. Sometimes things try my patience, but I always suggest one's goals can be achieved. You can make things happen if you really want to get there. I have seen many people with disabilities go on to fulfil their dreams - they are heroes and survivors. Whatever happens you can still do good things. You make your own decisions; you can make your life good or bad.

Unlike my parents, I will love my children till my last breath, and I hope people reading this will never stop loving their children.

My own mother was a cold, calculating person. I saw her destroy - not only with the razor - and feel nothing. She had the capacity to be cruel and so did my father who was silent and calculating and so sure of himself. I chose to bring up my children completely differently to them and my upbringing - with love.

I have never asked 'Why me?' I am a survivor of horror and have gone on to help, to show others that to take revenge, to hate or hurt, doesn't make you feel better. I've done what all survivors have done. Life goes on and I hope we learn from our mistakes.

As a child, I often lay in bed and wondered what sins I had committed that my family punished me so severely, and why I had been forsaken by the Guardian Angel and God who looked after little children. I actually didn't know what sins were; no-one had explained to me what represented a sin. I was Mary, just a naive child in a family of monsters. I'd carried a ton weight of guilt on my shoulders, but the 'code of silence' stayed with me. To defy it only brought more trouble and, as I grew older, threats to others in my family. My books, telling my life story, serve a purpose to many who have had similar dysfunctional lives.

Before my life ends I must say I do not forgive the Catholic nuns who took my mother's dirty donations of hush-money and turned a blind eye to my non-school attendance and, when I did attend, the odd way I walked due to the terrible treatment at home.

I do not forgive the Baptist church for knowingly performing a marriage to a reluctant bride – Mrs Buchanan had made a donation to ensure the priest asked no questions. I never saw or spoke with the minister until the church ceremony... wasn't that unusual?

Nor do I forgive The Salvation Army for allowing their members to lie and cheat under the pretence of Christian belief - not only Mrs Buchanan and her accomplices years ago, but even to this day. For years, I have worked with The Salvation Army doing what they aspire to do best, helping people in need. The annual Red Shield Appeal is The Salvation Army's signature fundraising drive which helps fund the vast network of social and community services and I have led many Appeals to great success.

One Christmas holiday, I gathered together a list of names of local needy children to receive the presents left under the Christmas tree at the local Kmart supermarket. These gifts were taken to a Salvation Army Captain where I lived for distribution, and I collected and delivered them to the families. This system worked well for two years but when I went to collect the toys the following year, two days before Christmas, this Captain informed me he wouldn't hand them over. He was of the opinion that a family, with a child on my list, had been 'double-dipping.' They had already visited the Salvation Army shop and been given a hamper – so all the children on my list were being made to suffer.

He would not change his mind and I went home empty-handed.

On learning this, people from the St Vincent De Paul Society, Lifeline, White Lady Funerals and Avon, stepped in with donated toys and every child on my list received a present. I understand that the K Mart presents were distributed amongst the hierarchy and friends of the local church, and I complained to the new officer, the previous one having retired to Sydney. When I requested a new badge to replace my ageing one, I was met with a barrage of contempt and refusal. When I expressed my disgust, I was told, 'How do I know you won't give The Salvation Army a bad name?'

My son heard the conversation and, annoyed with the way they had treated me, wrote to complain. I received an apology of lies from The Salvation Army - it was not sincere, stating the Officer had misunderstood me and they appreciated my work. Later on, they apologised for some of the awful things that had occurred and described the changes they had made there. However, I feel overall, things haven't changed much – they just updated their Salvation Army uniforms.

These so-called religious people have not been punished for the horror they knowingly inflicted on people. There are some who say this is not true but there are many of us who know that it is true - and carry the scars. Victims die but survivors live on, and Mary lived on – without turning to prostitution, drink, or drugs. Mary became Maria for a reason – to do good things; it is not the end.

And yes, dear reader, although I spent so many years unable to cry, I finally learned to shed tears. At forty I was finally brought to tears by my mother saying cruel things to me. But even today, all these years later, I weep inside and don't show emotion like most people. It was steadily bashed out of me as a child by my family and old habits don't fade easily.

When I look back on my life, I can't believe I'm eighty-nine. Where did the decades go? The years raced by and now I live on the Gold Coast. I've had many tragedies in my life – and I know I'm not alone, we all have them – so I just try to concentrate on helping people, so they too don't feel the hurt I felt.

The words I have spoken have been penned for me. It could not have been easy for the writer because no corners were to be cut - no white lies. If I couldn't remember it truthfully, it was left out. I described things as they were, not as I wished they were. I tried being the perfect wife and the perfect mother ... perhaps I shouldn't have tried so hard. My only advice is don't turn a blind eye. Don't let it happen again, dear reader. Don't let it happen again.

* * *

EPILOGUE

For those who wonder what happened to the people in my life, I mention them now :

Michele – my elder daughter, unable to cope with everyday life as a schoolgirl, continually ran away from home. Her awful father Lyall, and his Buchanan family, were monsters who raised her in their likeness. As she grew up we became friendlier, but she led her own life, and we didn't agree with her lifestyle. She had two lovely little children who she treated callously and created stories where she was never at fault. She didn't know how to be straight. She died in her sixties of liver cancer.

Melissa – my younger daughter (whisked away from me through The Salvation Army) and I, found one another. A Canberra public service family brought her up and told her she was adopted. They understood her to be the daughter of an Afro-Indian woman, so Melissa grew up thinking her birth mother and ancestors were Afro-Indian. She is caring and understanding, and we have developed a loving relationship. She's sixty-four years of age, and when she phones me, the sound of her voice and the manner she uses to speak with me, gives me an incredible feeling I find hard to explain. It's such a thrill. That my dear child has grown into a woman who is loving, and calls me 'Mum,' is just a wonderful feeling.

My eldest son – grew to become a darling, good-looking man – a loving and caring person, understanding and supportive. He is a treasure and does so much for me.

My middle son – grew up to be a kind, handsome and intelligent man. With his young life destroyed by the terrible things done to him at the United Protestant Association home (who acknowledged they had wrecked his childhood) it declined even further when a girlfriend became his government-paid carer. He had rescued Amanda who said she had been brutalised by everyone she came into contact with; later we found this to be completely untrue. I never tried to intervene, but as my son became sicker and sicker, Amanda started to have seizures. We found out later she had watered down his pain medicine, causing him terrible pain, and took his prescription drugs herself. His health deteriorated as she siphoned his medicine. One night this 'carer' took my son's car and crashed it, persuading him to purchase the replacement car in her name. Following his death, she cleared out everything I'd bought in the apartment and took off. Afterwards we found she had also been stealing money from his bank account to the tune of forty thousand dollars.

With the only witness gone, the police didn't feel we could bring a successful case to court against her, and, to my dismay, I understand she also received 'grief money' from Centrelink. My son died a few months before the UPA home made another substantial pay-out. Now each time I hear the name 'Amanda' I feel sick.

My youngest son – My Youngest son sadly turned into a stranger as the years past. I love all my three boys, but he retreated from our family and is uninterested in us all.

In later life it broke my heart when he read my first book and told me I should have written it under an alias - did that mean he was ashamed to be known as my son? It made me feel as though he was a class above us, his family. His behaviour hurt me deeply. The Scottish girl he married phoned me (one of the three times she ever contacted me over the years) upset about my first book and told me she could get the sack from her bank job because of it, which was ludicrous.

I found my son had turned into an indifferent, stranger, which shouldn't have surprised me as his father Tony was a monster and so were his brutish grandparents.

Tony – over the years, apart from the thugs he sent to intimidate me, has been completely uninterested in me and our sons. Our sons, in turn, knew he was their father as I had told them but, since he had never featured in their lives, they had no interest in him … except for my middle son. Being curious to meet his biological father, Eberhard and I drove him to Tony's house. We waited in the car, out of sight from the door, and my son – now a grown man – walked up the path, knocked on the door and told his father who he was. Tony didn't invite him in and kept him talking on the doorstep. Instead of owning up to taking advantage of a young girl who thought he was a single man, his father said, 'Oh yes – your mother and I were very foolish people.' After that, my son didn't want to stay even five minutes talking to this man who looked like him. He saw no rapport whatsoever between them, and turned and walked away, back to the car and out of Tony's life. Thankfully 'The Italian Club' note was the last I ever heard from Tony.

My brothers – we were never really 'family' so, except for the Victims of Crime letters, (they had suggested I sent letters to my monster brothers confronting them on their criminal acts to me) I have had no contact with them and nor do I wish to. However, despite his monstrous father, my nephew, Michael, is a wonderful man and we have become close.

Lyall Buchanan – married some lovely lady who divorced him – one can only guess why. He had heart trouble and died.

Mrs Buchanan – died of bowel cancer.

Joyce Buchanan – suffered from dementia and died in an old-people's home in Queensland. I went to visit her once, but she didn't recognise me. I had dearly loved her two little girls and they will never be forgotten by me. When I met one of them as an adult, she recalled knowing I was being badly treated. Growing up, she knew there was something 'not right' in the Buchanan household.

Patricia – moved to Western Australia and we corresponded by mail until she died there some years later - just a few months after Eberhard's death.

Frau Metchler – a friend of Eberhard's, a beautiful, wealthy lady, and the owner of The Parisian Pussy Cat restaurant in Sydney, continued to take care to keep the just-arrived, young European men, housed and safe and show them Australian ways - so they could fit in to Australian society.

Vera – the friend who named me Attara, the name I used as my stage name, ended up in India. One day, out of the blue I received a letter (which I still have to this day) from Kerala, India, where she had gone to teach dancing - I couldn't believe she was actually teaching the local men to dance. She asked me to come and join her. I had a husband and children so it was out of the question … but I often wonder what my life would have been like had I taken up her offer.

* * *

ACKNOWLEDGEMENTS

Thank you to todays Police force, the fact that these two books of mine would never have come out if it had not been for the Redcliffe Police, who caught red handed the person who was about to stab me because I had refused to pay extortion demands. It was the Police who got in touch with the Victims of Crime in the Valley Brisbane and it was there that a wonderful Counsellor finely helped me break the code of silence of my life.

The care and consideration that the Police of today give those in need of help, women need no longer be afraid of being ridiculed if they got to a Police station and any child in need of assistance will always find it a the Police stations of today.

I'm still in contact with the very first lady counsellor I opened up to – she did what she knew to do best. I finally broke the 'code of silence' and unlocked the memory of the horrors I'd had to live with for so many years. We are still in touch.

Because of my health issues I have had many wonderful doctors in my life, and I think of them often. I want to thank :

Dr Stulzman – he took me, a frightened, immature girl, and gradually gave me the gift of confidence to become a woman, keeping me alive with nutrition injections and helping me open up my life to the real world.

Professor Lawrence Hirst – whose operation saved my sight. Sight is so important, and I've never forgotten him. Without that operation I would not have been able to write these books.

Dr Andrew Childs – his operation on me at Sydney's St George Hospital gave me many more years of life and I'm very grateful for his expertise.

Dr Steven Stylian – a wonderful Oncologist and a true Christian.

Dr Nic Crampton – a surgeon and my hero.

Dr Marian Evans – I would not feel good if I did not mention my doctor in Tugun, Queensland. She has gone a step further than most doctors who have cared for my health in these last few harrowing years, and I'm so grateful. She's one of the few doctors I can trust to understand the trauma I've had in my life.

I must say special thanks to:

Ralph James – a top criminal lawyer, my treasured friend and solicitor - a wonderful man of integrity with a beautiful family. Over many years, he always found the time to care and support me, to ensure my family and I were protected - forever my friend.

Andy McDermott (Publicious Book Publishing) – thank you for believing in me. You've gone 'above and beyond' to help me with my books.

Anna – the Angel has become a dear friend who I still see regularly and I'm so happy she came into my life and put her stamp on my first book. She has helped me with this book too and she really is an angel.

David and Dot Smith – I thank you from the depth of my heart for allowing me to share in the joy of your Angel daughter Anna. You taught her well and gave her the gift of true caring and compassion, it is important for the survival of mankind.

John – last but not forgotten. He was introduced by my son Leo whilst they both worked in Community Care. He became a foster son who, whilst not having the family's 'tall' genes, was always there for me. Thank you for all you do.

Terry Spring – thank you Terry for writing my recorded memories and for finding out historical information about my mother. could never be sure how much of my mother's recollections of her past were true – she always told people what she wanted them to think. We learned that, at four years-old, my mother and her older sister Mary, were 'taken into care' whilst living with their prostitute mother in the NSW country town of Narromine. The sisters were separated, and the next information was a 1914 Police Gazette pronouncing my sixteen-year-old mother missing from a Paddington girls' home. Despite searching her whole life, my mother never located her sister Mary, but she ensured she changed her name so many times, the runaway girl in the white dress and black shoes was never found.

And finally, thank *you* for reading my story. If you found it interesting, I would greatly appreciate a short review on Amazon or Goodreads. You may also want to read my first book about my childhood, *Daughter of The Razor*, which can be found in all major online bookstores.

* * *

FINALLY

This is a personal thank you to John Laws, a true Australian personality who, in his kindness, supported and promoted my first book 'Daughter of the Razor' and gave me encouragement for this second book 'The Rescue.' He showed real care and support to a survivor. Mr laws, I thank you.

* * *

www.ingramcontent.com/pod-product-compliance
Lightning Source LLC
Chambersburg PA
CBHW060352090426

42734CB00011B/2119